DANGEROUS LIVES

DANGEROUS LIVES

CARL GLASSMAN

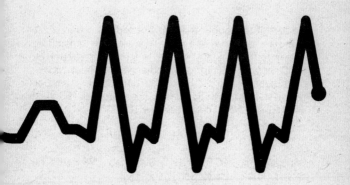

SCHOLASTIC BOOK SERVICES
New York Toronto London Auckland Sydney Tokyo

Acknowledgments

Thanks to all those who took the time to share their stories and feelings about their work; and to the New York City Police Department, the National Aeronautics and Space Administration, and The Big Apple Circus for their cooperation.

Special thanks, of course, to April Koral.

ISBN 0-590-30875-0

12 11 10 9 8 7 6 5 4 3 2 1   11   9/7 0 1 2 3 4/8

For Pa

CONTENTS

INTRODUCTION

Most people make a point of avoiding danger. A fearless few make danger their business. For the policeman defusing a bomb or the war correspondent dodging bullets, the pilot testing a new plane, or the movie stunt performer plunging off a building, staying alive is a full-time job. The rest of us, standing safely to the side, marvel at their skills, thrill to their deeds, and shudder at the danger. Sometimes we even call them crazy.

The people in this book are not suicidal, they're not daredevils and, rest assured, they're not crazy. Without their wits, they wouldn't have lived to tell their stories.

Talking to them, it's easy to forget that there's anything dangerous about their lives— they can describe the most harrowing adventure as calmly as we talk about the weather.

Strangest of all, where we see peril, they see safety. The race-car driver, test pilot, and movie stunt performer like to stress that there's much less risk to their jobs now than in years past. The circus aerialist says he is more comfortable high in the air than on solid ground.

The men and women you will read about are as different from each other as are their professions. But they share an important trait: towering self-confidence. If at first they seem immodestly sure of themselves, remember that self-doubt is one of the biggest hazards of a hazardous job. If you think you can't dismantle that bomb in time, or turn that corner at 180 miles an hour, you'll prove yourself right. Remember, too, that the confidence they bring to their work is based on training, practice, and skill.

The driving force behind those who lead dangerous lives is rarely just money or recognition. More often it is a love for their work that borders on obsession. Even if common sense told them to quit, they probably could not.

Neither death nor injury to their colleagues is enough to make them think twice about their professions. Nor, usually, are the fears and worries of family members. John Young, an astronaut who's flown in space more times than any other man, speaks of his wife's jitters as though they were a fact of life. "She used to work in the missile program and she's seen a few new missiles blow up," he says. "I keep telling her this is not the same thing but she's not convinced." A beginning trapeze artist sadly describes how her parents feel about her new career. "They're not too happy about it. My mother is always having nightmares. My father is a little calmer."

Yet when asked why they flirt with danger— when most people play it safe—the men and women interviewed for this book were hard-pressed for an explanation. Some deny they risk their lives at all, saying they're just ordinary people doing a difficult job well. Others say they find reward in the risk. "Maybe because we're prepared to die, we appreciate things a little bit more," notes race-car driver, Bobby Rahall. "Maybe we feel that the quality of life is better than the quantity."

Finally, there are a handful who simply like the sheer excitement. "There's nothing more stimulating," says former war correspondent Mike Ross, "than being shot at and missed."

DANGEROUS LIVES

STUNT PERFORMERS

Vic Magnotta gets killed for a living. With regularity, he dies in crashes, smashes, falls, fights, and fires—or so it seems on the silver screen. As a professional stuntman, Magnotta has been the blood, guts, and backbone of 126 action movies and more TV shows than he can remember, doing everything from wing-walking to plunging cars into 25 feet of water. So far, Magnotta has bounced back every time. But what makes the risk and rigor worth it?

"Granted, there's a certain amount of exhibitionism and macho that comes into play," says Magnotta, a former Notre Dame running back and ex-Marine. "All stunt performers are actors. They love to be in the limelight. They love to do their bit, get it right, and get the applause. Many times we do a stunt and the crew responds favorably by applauding. But as far as going out there and putting on a show for everyone, I never look at it from that point of view. I'm there to do a job and I want to do it to the best of my ability."

Then there's the pay. It's quick and generous. A stuntman or stuntwoman can earn a day's base pay — usually $325 — plus a stunt adjustment or bonus for working as little as 30 minutes. In fact, he may perform on the sets of three movies or TV shows in one week — never hanging around long enough to find out the plot of any of them.

The bonus pay varies greatly, depending on the skills and the risks involved. For example, a stunt performer who is "simply" hit by a car going 15 miles an hour might charge $300. But if his assignment is to be hit by a car going 25 miles an hour, which in turn sends him flying onto the hood and through a breakaway windshield, his fee could be as high as $800. (In a year, the average stuntman earns $60,000 to $75,000.)

Magnotta's biggest payday came in 1976, for an unsuccessful movie called *The Slightly Damaged Man,* in which he jumped eight stories while fully covered in flames (he was wearing an asbestos suit and mask). His bill for that moment of madness: $15,000.

"My main concern was whether there were any wind currents in the alley that could make me drift. Eight stories is a long way coming down. I wanted to make sure I hit the air bag just right."

On the set of *Somebody Killed Her Husband*, stuntman Vic Magnotta confers with Jimmy Halligan, the man he hires to design and make special rigging that is critical to his safety during high work. "I've put my life in his hands many times and I don't even think about it," says Magnotta. (S.J. Esposito)

There was more to it than that. The last moments before the jump, Magnotta took deep breaths to conserve the self-contained air in his suit. Just before the director yelled, "Roll it," rubber cement was smeared over the back of his suit and, with headgear in place, over the top of his head. "Once they lock you in you can't see where you're going. The eye holes fog up. They lit me and then I timed it so the steps were just right. I knew exactly how many steps I had to take before I started my fall. In the air you can't see where you have to roll [into position for a safe landing] and you just about have to imagine where you are by counting. It worked out just great."

Although the price of a stunt is frequently geared to the degree of danger, stuntmen like Magnotta insist there's really no danger in their work — as long as their skills are in place and the proper safety precautions are taken. "Otherwise," he admits, "you're just going to get yourself killed."

Magnotta recalls being asked, along with stuntman Glen Wilder, to drive a car off a bridge into a lake, a stunt he considers comparatively simple. "We said, 'Sure, no problem, we'll do it.' We told them our requirements (a backup crew, four scuba divers, tow trucks, two mechanics, plus rigging for the car) and how much it would cost them—$50,000. They said no, that it was too much money, that they'd pay $5,000." Magnotta refused. "Somehow they picked up two guys who were quote unquote stuntmen—and there are a lot of guys going around saying they're stuntmen; a lot of them are daredevils, a lot of them are stupid. These two guys drove the car into the water, and they drowned.

"A lot of producers try to nickel-and-dime you. And in a situation like that you just walk away. If they're going to be cheap in this aspect of it, they're going to be cheap right down the line, and I'm going to get hurt. My life is more important than becoming a daredevil."

Regardless of how dangerous a stunt may appear, Magnotta claims that safety is always the number-one priority and that very little is left to chance.

"For me to do a stunt, I must be able to control ninety percent of it. If I can't control it, I won't do it. It's as simple as that. There's that ten percent gap there that I don't control. But I feel, with my athletic background and with the backup crew I have working with me, I can compensate for it."

So how does Magnotta muster that kind of self-confidence with a tough stunt he's never done before? He found himself in that situation when he doubled for Judd Hirsch in the movie *King of the Gypsies*. The stunt: getting a "shotgun blast" in the chest, followed by a backward fall 52 feet to the ground.

"A backfall is one of the most difficult because you can't see where you're going," Magnotta explains. "You can try to cheat and look where you're going, but when you have such a short distance, you're down in no time flat." Because he had never fallen backwards from such a height, Magnotta practiced by falling shorter distances onto an airbag he set up inside a gym. "I went through the thing a million times in my head so when I actually did the stunt it was anti-climactic.

"I take into account every possible thing that can go wrong. For example, if while going off I tripped a little bit to the side, then I know to drop that right arm to compensate for the balance so I don't start to tumble. It's the same thing I did as a football player. Before every game I would spend two hours going over every single play."

Magnotta claims that only once in his 15-year career, in a scene for *Kojak,* did he approach a stunt without "complete and total confidence." The task was to drive a car onto a ramp, flip it over completely, and land it right side up—not an unusual stunt, but a first for Magnotta. "I was really nervous about the whole thing," he recalls. "It was probably the only time I can honestly say I did not control the stunt ninety percent. I knew exactly what I needed in the car to get it rigged and I knew exactly what I had to do on the ramp to get it up high enough to flip it, but I had never done that."

Was it safety that worried Magnotta about doing the new trick? Not in the least, he says, just the possibility of embarrassing himself by getting it wrong. "I had double rollbars in the car, six point harnesses, a safety unit standing by with extinguishers in case the car broke into flames. I was just worried that I might not be able to flip it over properly."

Magnotta can spin cars 180 and 360 degrees on a dime, roll them, put them up on two wheels, and safely crash them. Still, he says, "I don't think of myself as a car expert. I would say that's my weakest area."

"Weak" may seem too harsh a word, but in the ultra-competitive stunt performer's world, versatility is the key to success. All skills, from high falls to scuba diving, must be mastered. "They want people who can do everything," Magnotta says.

Magnotta was training to be a stuntman even before he knew it. As a teenager he played most school sports, loved horseback riding, and thought nothing of making 75-foot cliff dives into water. In 1962, friends of his family recommended him to a producer of the *Daniel Boone* TV series, who was able to use Magnotta's horseback riding skills.

Working summers in Hollywood more than paid his tuition at Notre Dame. With an eye toward eventually producing movies, he earned a Master's degree in communications at New York University. The next two and a half years were spent with the Marines Special Forces, learning things such as helicopter repelling and scuba diving (for planting underwater mines in Vietnam). And on his own, just for fun, he mastered wing-walking. All of these

7

skills would later become invaluable to him as a stuntman.

After his stint in the service, Magnotta went back to school for a second Master's degree, this time in physical education, specializing in kinesiology (the study of the mechanics of body movements) and physiology. Returning to movies, he worked not only as a stuntman but also served behind the scenes on 42 films as a stunt coordinator, creating and engineering the action sequences.

Magnotta believes he joined his profession at the end of an era. The people who gave stunt performers the image of drinking, brawling, and unthinking daredevils were finally vanishing from the scene. When a colleague, believed to be working under the influence of drugs, died on the *Daniel Boone* show in the early '60s, Magnotta never forgot it.

"In the scene the guy was on a buckboard, the horses running wild toward the edge of the cliff. The horses broke loose and the buckboard headed toward the cliff by itself. The guy was supposed to jump out, but his timing was off and he went over the cliff and got killed. That scared the living daylights out of me.

"The old concept of a stuntman being a drunk, and having to get juiced and filled with pills before he could do a stunt — that's over with. If I'm going to be balancing off a 26-story building or hanging off the wing of an airplane or repelling out of a helicopter 200 feet up, there's no way I would even consider touching a drop of liquor. My reflexes have to be razor sharp."

It is not surprising that pain-killing drugs and alcohol figured in the lives of many of the movies' early stunt performers. In the beginning years of motion pictures, stuntmen and stuntwomen were a motley group of steeplejacks, prize fighters, circus clowns, tumblers, rodeo riders, and vaudeville actors, who lacked the training and expertise of today's professionals. And, without powerful unions to back them up, stunt performers were forced to carry out the director's every whim. The choice was often to do a risky stunt or not work at all. Accidents were an accepted part of the job and careers were often cut short by serious injury or death. Few stunt performers lasted more than five years.

During their silent years, movies especially depended on the somewhat violent antics of slapstick comedy and the action in thrillers to make up for the lack of sound. Men and women flocked to Hollywood to fill the stunt rolls and earn quick bucks. Each tried to outdo the other by undertaking more spectacular—and therefore more dangerous—stunts.

Without the use of elaborate special effects, camera angles, and safety devices, the first stunt performers were forced to rely almost entirely on their own skills to get themselves safely through dangerous scenes. That was especially true because audiences and directors demanded realism. One stuntman, for example, decided to create a realistic fight scene by hiding a five-dollar gold piece in his pocket and telling the other stuntmen that it belonged to anyone who could get it.

In the 1936 film *Darkest Africa*, director B. Reeves Eason (known as Breezy) nearly killed stuntman-animal trainer Clyde Beatty for the sake of realism. The director demanded that Beatty wrestle a "trained" lion with his bare hands, despite Beatty's protest that he was not experienced with such a dangerous feat.

Here's how Beatty explained the bout, as described 10 years later in the book, *Jungle Performers*:

> The day came. The cannibals hurled me into the pit. Remembering that this was supposed to be a wrestling match, I was planning to limit myself to a few toe-holds and half-nelsons. But as I got to my feet it became clear that Bobby (the tiger) had not bothered to learn wrestling rules. He charged at me with his eyes narrowed and blazing, jaws wide open. When he got close, he reared and clubbed at me with his enormous claws. Clearly the jungle atmosphere and the fact that he didn't know me had combined to drive Bobby temporarily berserk. Presently he was right on top of me.... With the full force of my right fist, I belted him squarely on the chin, at the same time letting out a mur-

Magnotta plunges out a window and onto an airbag for a scene from *King of the Gypsies*. (Michael Cardacino)

derous yell which distracted him a little. Dazed slightly by my blow, he plunged backwards momentarily, then recovered and came back at me, roaring with rage. I had only made him angrier.... As he slammed his paws down on my shoulders I managed to let go another right-hand punch. In my terror I began shouting like a crazy man. The cage attendants suddenly seemed to discover that I wasn't kidding after all, and rattled the door. Bobby by now was hugging me with his paws and I shot punches weakly at his stomach with my free left hand, my right hand being pinioned to my side by his paws. Old wounds on that side began to burn, a recently healed cut in my right hand was reopened and blood oozed tricklingly out. My legs ached and I felt sick. Still the attendants rattled the door and finally the noise caught Bobby's attention. He pricked up his ears, sprang toward the door, and bolted out. This old device often works with animals; they associate the rattle of the door with food.... I leaned against the cage, panting, perspiring, and marveling at how close I had been to death. Breezy Eason leaned down from the top of the pit where he and the cameraman were perched in safety. "Boy, that was swell!" said Breezy excitedly. "Get your breath, Clyde, and we'll do a retake...."

Between 1925 and 1930, more than 10,000 performers, mostly stunt performers, were injured during Hollywood filming. Fifty-five of them died. Usually, studios tried to keep the casualties secret in order to maintain a clean image. However, Fox Studios capitalized on the death of a stunt pilot killed during the film of The Skywayman (1920) by widely publicizing that 10 percent of the film's profits would go to the dead man's family.

To add insult to a multitude of injuries, not only weren't stunt performers named in movie credits, but studios often disclaimed using them at all, giving full heroic credit to their stars. (A stunt performer was not presented an Academy Award until 1966.) And although by the late 1920s they were paid well ($50 a day), much of that money often went toward paying for their own crew and equipment. When injured, the performers also paid for their own medical treatment.

Still, producers had more than enough stunt performers to choose from, many of whom were willing to add to the risk by exercising dangerously little caution. The old-timers merrily rolled stock cars without rollbars, and neglected to spot-weld the doors to help seal them shut. For a 1922 movie, one stuntman did a 55-mile-an-hour ramp jump, protected only by a rolled-up overcoat between his chest and the steering column. High-fall artists dropped onto flimsy carpets, held up fireman-style by assistants. (Today, giant airbags act as the stunt performer's crash pad for the highest jumps.)

With or without proper precautions, many stunt performers simply couldn't say no to the director's wildest commands. One extreme case was high-fall specialist Richard Talmadge, who gave this account back in 1945 of a stunt he agreed to undertake for no understandable reason.

"A car in which I was jumping a ditch had turned over in midair and I was flung out 25 feet. I had to go on crutches for three weeks. Universal was making a serial and they wanted me badly for a stunt. I told them I was a cripple but they insisted I should try—they were in a spot and no else would do. So I was hoisted up 40 feet onto a little ledge on a tower. I threw the crutches away and just stood there for a few minutes. I was so stiff I could hardly move. I was supposed to jump and land on a bunch of mattresses in a dry riverbed. I jumped—but the property man had decided that I would land a few feet farther to the left and had moved the mattress. I landed in the riverbed with a terrific thud. They thought I was dead. But I got up—and walked off without crutches. The fall had straightened out my bad back. It was quite a fall! The imprint of my body was clearly visible in the riverbed."

The Making of a Stunt

It's early evening on a Queens, New York,

street. Down the block a fog machine is busy chugging away, and through the mist the movie camera catches one take after another of a street gang chasing "Turkey," a rival gang member played by Alan Rosenberg. At the other end of the street, where the air is clear and the evening is quiet, stunt coordinator Vic Magnotta surveys a section of an elevated subway platform. Mark Sutton, 25, dressed in black jacket, black pants, black boots, and a pasty bald wig—a dead ringer at a distance for Turkey—approaches Magnotta with a smile.

"How do you feel?" Vic asks him.

"Good," Sutton replies with confidence. "I'm ready for it."

What Sutton, who's acting as Rosenberg's double, is ready for is to climb the vertical support girder to the top of the "el," step off onto a horizontal pipe, grab a rope hanging from the dark underside of the platform, and fall backwards some 20 feet. The fall will be the fatal climax to the chase scene being filmed down the street.

The scene, from *The Wanderers,* will be just one stunt among countless others seen in the next year's crop of action movies. A quick thrill quickly forgotten. Though not unusually daring or spectacular, it will require enough planning and safety precautions to put the Boy Scouts to shame. Rookie stuntman Sutton, appearing in his very first movie, will be directed by Magnotta. As stunt coordinator for the film, it's Magnotta's job to choreograph the fall, and see

15

to it that Sutton walks away unhurt.

In the final, edited version of the movie, Sutton's stunt follows by only seconds the action now being shot. But in reality, tonight, it will not occur for another six hours. As those long hours pass, Magnotta will become increasingly concerned that all the standing around will dull Mark's reflexes when the moment finally comes. But for now he's glad for the extra time to rehearse.

Like most stunts, there will be no dry runs. The real thing happens only before the rolling cameras — and preferably only once. Sutton can only simulate the fall from a short height. Across the street from the site, Magnotta sets up a stepladder with a blue crash pad lying behind it. Mark climbs to the top. Two spotters, on hand to catch him if he misses his mark, are on each side. Another extends his hand to Sutton, who grips it with both of his as if it were the rope he'll be holding before he falls.

"Get your feet wide, as wide as you can," Magnotta tells him. "On impact you gotta tuck it up — keep your head tucked in. No neck whips here."

Magnotta knows that Sutton knows how to fall, but he will repeat the instructions a hundred times. Safety is number one.

Sutton plunges backwards once, then again and again, each time with feedback from Magnotta. "There, you got it...that's it, one more time...okay, you turned that time ... good ... now you turned a little bit to your right. No big deal...." Magnotta's commands are short, direct, and reassuring. He's not making a movie now, he's coaching an athlete.

After some 20 falls Magnotta orders the mat put away, but the practice will go on and on. "I know he can do it," Magnotta says, walking back across the street to the rear end of a rented equipment truck where Sutton will rehearse his moves some more. With a first-time stunt, he explains, it's either "super perfect" or it falls apart completely.

"When I was a kid I used to do mountain climbing," actor Alan Rosenberg was saying as he, Magnotta, and Sutton walked toward the crew bus. "Now I'm scared of heights." Although Rosenberg won't be making the fall, he will have to scamper up the "el" girder before the camera, which he's not looking forward to doing. But Magnotta has a device to help relieve his fears. Inside the bus, he shows Rosenberg how to install a strap, which ties around the waist and crotch. At the end of the strap is a clip that can fasten around one of the ladder rungs and hold him securely in case he has to stay up on the ladder for any length of time, or gets panicky and feels like he might fall. All he has to do is unzip his pants, pull out the strap, and hook himself on. Rosenberg and Sutton both strap themselves in — before the bug-eyed gazes of some teenagers peeking through the windshield—and head back to the set.

"Ahhh," Rosenberg gasps as he looks up at Sutton who is hanging from the top rung of the girder. "Seeing him do it scares *me*," he says. Standing beside Rosenberg are Magnotta and the film's director, Phil Kaufman (who directed *The Invasion of the Body Snatchers*, 1978), who wants to get an idea of what the stunt will look like. Magnotta explains that Sutton will climb from the girder onto a horizontal bar before falling.

"Show me," says the director.

"I don't want him to go out there without his crash pad set up yet," Magnotta tells him. "He could lose his grip."

Sutton climbs down and Magnotta takes aside two stuntmen, dressed as rival gang members, who will serve as spotters when Rosenberg makes his climb, and when Sutton falls.

"Right now he's cool," Magnotta says. "But when they start to shoot and the adrenaline starts to flow he could get a little shaky." In the event that part of Sutton's body misses the crash pad, he explains, their job is to act as a "safety valve" by diving beneath him and scooping him onto the mat.

"The best part of making a movie is the food," Sutton says as he sits down with a plate full of roast beef and rice in the back room of a café where cast and crew have gathered for their catered dinner at nine-thirty. Someone walking by the table tells Mark that they hope they don't see his meal again when he makes his fall later that night. It's a joke, but Sutton decides he really didn't want roast beef after all, and just eats the rice.

Sutton, a graduate of the University of Colorado and a stunt school in California, remains quiet for much of the time leading to his fall—perhaps partly due to nerves and partly to concentrating on the task ahead. "The mind has to be totally relaxed," says the stuntman, who spent the previous day working out on a trampoline and doing back dives into a pool. "Before I do a stunt I go over it hundreds and hundreds of times in my mind. Then, when I finally perform, I'm able to block everything out."

Enrico, the makeup man, is touching up Sutton's bald head, which by now looks like lumpy Silly Putty, while Rosenberg does six takes racing up the girder. With each try he gains more confidence, getting a little more daring and hamming it up with an extra slip of the foot or a terrified groping for the rungs.

It's eleven-ten now, and Magnotta says they may not get to the stunt tonight. There are still the close-ups to be made of Turkey's frightened face and the shots of the rival gang members as they make their menacing approach in the final scene.

But at midnight Rosenberg gets the final "All right, cut it, that's nice, Alan," from the director, and Magnotta takes his place, climbing

Attempting to set a new world record, movie stuntman A.J. Bakunas plunges 22 stories—323 feet—onto a 30 by 40 foot airbag. The airbag burst on impact and Bakunas was killed. (UPI)

to the top of the girder to show Sutton the pre-fall choreography. Drop the right leg, then replant it. Drop the right arm. Drop the left arm. As it comes down, fall back. Then Sutton goes up, repeating Magnotta's movements.

A pick-up arrives, crammed with unfolded cardboard boxes and two crash pads tied on top. Grips (the men who construct and move things about on the set) begin making them into boxes while Magnotta places about 50 of them, two deep, where Sutton will fall, and ties the bunch together with rope. The crash pads go on top.

Magnotta drills Sutton some more. "Jockey into position, drop that leg—you know exactly where it's going back to. Don't push off, I don't want you to push. Let the right arm down then let go. Don't look down. If I see your face you ruin the shot."

This time Sutton is practicing from the back of a trailer, falling back into Magnotta's arms.

"Any questions now?" he asks the stuntman. Sutton shakes his head no.

Still Magnotta has him practice it again.

"One more time now. You got it...one more time...."

A girl with a walkie-talkie approaches Magnotta.

"Vic, are you set?"

"We're all set," he replies.

"Quickly," a grip snaps.

"We're ready, chief," Magnotta tells the director.

The makeup man does a last-minute touch-up to Sutton's head, gluing the nape of his neck back down.

It's one-twenty in the morning and the set is being lit for the fall. Two cameras go into position near the mat; the one for slow motion is hand-held. The director of photography asks for a lens and Sutton does some deep knee-bends. Magnotta fills even these final moments with some quiet coaching.

Enrico, who sports a goatee and thin waxed mustache, paces about the set with paintbrush in one hand and a tube of red stuff in the other, looking like an artist in search of a canvas. He is called to apply a gash to the corner of Sutton's mouth.

"All right, here we go. Ladder, please." Sutton uses the ladder to sidestep the boxes blocking the girder's bottom rungs and climbs to the top.

"Move into place," Magnotta tells him.

A train roars by overhead and everyone freezes in place, waiting for it to pass. Then the fog machine coughs up some more mist.

"Stand by."

"Action, Mark," says Magnotta. There's reassurance in his voice.

Sutton falls. His body slaps the pad, then lies motionless.

From behind the ropes, where a gallery of spectators has dwindled to a handful, someone claps.

Mark sits up and moves off the mat as production people whisper privately. Magnotta pats him on the back and, wrapping his arm around the stuntman's shoulder, takes him off to the side. There will be a second take.

Sutton climbs back up. "Ready," someone says. "Ready to roll."

Magnotta calls action and Sutton drops. Again a deathly silence as he lies still on the mat.

"That was better," one cameraman says to the other. "Much better."

It's over. Sutton stands alone, seemingly in a fog of his own as he blankly watches the crew clear away his landing site.

"How was it?" someone asks him.

Sutton's face loosens and he grins.

"A piece of cake," he says.

AERIALISTS

For more than eight years now, Warren Bacon has made his living in midair, doing twists and turns and somersaults, walking high wires up to 185 feet above the ground, and otherwise risking his life as routinely as most people brush their teeth. As a circus aerialist, Bacon goes to work knowing that the tiniest error, the slightest mis-timing, could mean serious injury or death to him or his partner.

For all that, in Bacon's world there is no such thing as fright. He won't even use the word, admitting at worst to a very occasional case of "excessive apprehension."

"There are two types of fear," says Bacon, who now works as both a trainer and performer in New York's Big Apple Circus. "One is the paralyzing type of terror. The other type of fear is a healthy respect for the inherent risks of

The death-defying Wallendas perform their "human pyramid." In 1962 the pyramid collapsed. Two members of the family died and two others were seriously injured. (UPI)

what you are doing. I have never had that paralyzing type of fear of being in the air. I am perfectly at home. As a matter of fact, I'm much more comfortable in the air than I am on the ground. I'm a klutz on the ground. I trip over my own feet."

Bacon first discovered his aerial ease while at work on a Master's degree in molecular biology at Florida State University. From the age of 16 he had been an expert gymnast, winning several regional titles. And at Florida State he took time out from his studies to coach the gymnastics team. There he met Adrian Catarzi, a circus performer and member of an internationally famous family of bareback riders. It took little persuasion on Catarzi's part to convince Bacon to try out his skills in the air. With perfect calm, he climbed the rigging, and took to the trapeze like a parakeet to its perch.

Catarzi taught Bacon the art of "flying," of hurling from one swinging trapeze and being caught by a partner hanging from another. Each day, at the university's circus facilities, Catarzi coached Bacon for hours on the trapeze. And when the student finally returned to the ground, there were more hours to spend talking over each movement of the flying act, drilling it into Bacon's brain, over and over and over, like an actor learning his lines.

Bacon did get his Master's degree, but decided to trade his lab coat for leotards and make the circus his life. "I'd always loved the circus as a spectator," he recalls. "I was totally enchanted — whether it was a little one-ring mud show or Ringling Brothers.''

The rookie aerialist earned his wings in both arenas. Moving from one flying act to another, he performed in tiny towns and county fairs across the country, all the while building his strength and skills. With Ringling Brothers he was the only non-family member to perform with the Gaonas, considered the greatest flying act in this country.

Bacon didn't think of himself as being especially daring until he went to work for a thrill show in Taiwan. There, the producers of a TV show called *The Thrill Seekers,* narrated by Chuck Connors, decided to do a 30-minute segment about him.

"It never dawned on me that anyone would consider what I do as dangerous," he says. "It had always seemed an extension of gymnastics."

It is probably no wonder that Bacon, like many other circus performers, takes his skills — and the accompanying risks — for granted. After all, his whole world is the circus. There's little time or opportunity to meet the "towners," the ordinary folks who come to see the shows and marvel at the stunts. Instead, his closest friends are people who think nothing of poking their heads inside the mouths of lions, jumping through hoops of fire, or walking high wires stretched between skyscrapers.

"The circus performer is not an unusual person," he says. "He possesses no extraordinary

27

Karl Wallenda inches his way across a high wire above San Francisco's Candlestick Park. (Wide World Photos)

trait. We are ordinary people who perhaps have subjected ourselves to a little more stringent type of self-discipline than the average person."

The self-discipline he refers to is not just the hard, repetitious work needed to learn new tricks, but the self-discipline of overcoming an even bigger monster: pain.

All circus performers must accept pain as part of the job. Rope burns, jammed fingers, sprains and strains, and a general condition of muscle soreness are not dramatic injuries, but they are the invisible torments that performers frequently suffer as they appear to glide through routines with the greatest of ease.

"You see a flyer miss a trick and land in a net. The net seems all soft and bouncy," says Bacon. "I still have scars on my back—major rope burns — where I ripped out of the catcher's hand and skidded down the net. In order to stop you, that net has to be very tight. And it's like running into a brick wall. It can knock the wind out of you. You land in the net on your head and you can break your neck. You land standing up in the net and you're going to break both legs."

But it's the resiliency of the aerialist's spirit — not his body — that allows him to bounce back from an injury. Take Bacon's accident of 1976. While working with the Gaona flying act with Ringling Brothers, his partner was supposed to have flown up from a swinging trapeze, perform a double somersault, and come back down to be caught by Bacon, who was swinging by the knees from another trapeze. Instead of his partner flying up, he shot "straight across at about 90 miles an hour" and hit him square in the face.

The impact immediately knocked Bacon unconscious, but there was still that split-second feeling of helplessness before the crushing blow. "I knew it was coming," Bacon recalls. "I knew I'd get hurt. A lot of times on a long trick you can get out of the way. But this was a line drive. There was no place to go because I was swinging into him."

Bacon fell limply into the net and when he came to, he was being treated for two jaw fractures and four misplaced teeth. For the next six weeks he dined in the hospital on baby food and mashed potatoes. Had it not been for sedatives he was given the day he left the hospital, he would have worked that day. Instead, he waited until the next day, when there were no nurses around to bother him with little things like pain-killers. "It was painful, initially," Bacon says now, with obvious understatement, "but it was more important that I work."

For the outsider, it's hard to understand why broken bones don't shatter ambitions under the bigtop. Even when a fellow performer is killed, aerialists allow themselves little time for reflection on their own death-defying lives. Self-doubt can be dangerous, for it leads to fear, which in turn fuels the risk of error. When

The 74-year-old Wallenda struggles to regain his balance during a high-wire walk in Puerto Rico. Seconds later the wirewalker fell 100 feet to his death, ending one of the most daring and distinguished lives in circus history. (Photo copyright by Gary Williams of *El Nueva Dia* via Wide World Photos)

74-year-old Karl Wallenda, the all-time greatest high-wire-walker, was thrown to his death by a gust of wind as he walked a wire strung 100 feet above a San Juan, Puerto Rico, street in 1978, his family went on to perform that very night.

"I cried when Karl died," says Warren Bacon, who knew the wire-walker. "The emotion I felt wasn't because he had fallen but because the circus had lost one of its truly great performers. But it has to go on. That happens. People fall. But because people fall, we don't quit. You get back up, if you can, and try again. If someone's killed it hurts you, but you put that aside."

If the death of a friend makes you reconsider your own career, Bacon adds, "then it's time to get out of the business."

The death of Karl Wallenda ended a 60-year career of unimaginable risk, perhaps the most artfully daring life in circus history. Like most European-born performers, Wallenda inherited, rather than chose, his circus profession. His grandfather, also named Karl, became the first of the death-defying Wallendas in 1874, when he began an act with 12 vicious Russian wolves. The next generation worked as aerialists. Karl's father remained in a flying act until he was 65, then retired to Africa where he caught big game for shipment to European zoos.

Karl Wallenda first walked the high wire in

public at the age of 16. But the feat offered little thrill or distinction for him, so despite warnings from others he designed a specially rigged bicycle and learned to ride across the high wire, his brother Herman balanced on his shoulders. By the time he was 18, Karl was cycling his brother across the Oder River at Breslau, Germany, 80 feet above the water.

In time, Herman grew too heavy for the act and Karl placed a "help wanted" ad for "a young girl who can work the ropes and has courage." The woman he hired was a 96-pound, fourth-generation aerialist named Helen Kreis—later to become Helen Wallenda. Many years down the road, after several family deaths and injuries, Helen would beg Karl to give up his daredevil routines, and while he performed she would sit alone in back rooms and pray. In those early days the pair struggled together for bookings, since most circus proprietors feared the Wallendas would fall, injuring spectators and provoking law suits. The performers were sleeping in a park in Havana, Cuba, without enough money to return to Europe, when John Ringling heard about them and brought the couple to the United States.

Unfortunately, the Wallendas are often remembered as much for their mishaps and tragedies as they are for their unparalleled scientific precision. But it is in the face of falls and failures that their self-discipline and determination have been best revealed.

In 1934, a heavy rain loosened the ground

33

that anchored the Wallendas' high-wire rigging. As the four-person pyramid inched across it on two bicycles, the wire slackened. There was a pause, a tremble, and then the great act fell.

In his book, *The Big Top—My 40 Years With the Greatest Show On Earth,* Fred Bradna gives this firsthand account of the incredible incident.

"I was near the bandstand, checking the readiness of the following act. Almost instinctively I called to Mickey Graves, the boss property man, 'Mickey, the Wallendas are falling.' He reacted instantly, and rushed with a crew of five and a portable net to the center ring, while bicycles and steel balancing poles crashed about him.

"The Wallendas did not come down. With astonishing presence of mind, Karl seized the wire with his hands and, as Helen fell past him, thrust his legs and caught her head in an ankle scissors hold. His grip was so firm that Helen lost consciousness from the pressure. Meanwhile, Herman had also caught the wire and Joseph, in passing him, had squirmed over for a perfect leg catch. Herman went hand over hand along the wire to the platform, dangling Joseph below him. Unable to resort to this maneuver lest Helen slip from between his locked ankles, Karl held her until the safety net was spread, then released her a moment later and followed her down. Neither was hurt.

"There is something peculiar about circus audiences which cause them to ignore accidents of a kind. I whistled in the next act, the music changed, and within seconds the spectators were engrossed in a new feature. Only those who previously had witnessed the Wallenda act seemed to know that this was not all just part of the show. The Wallendas worked that night as usual, Herman with a throat cut from his collision with the wire, Helen with a bandaged head."

The Wallendas' luck held firm until a January evening in Detroit, 1962, when they performed their most famous act: the seven-person pyramid. Four men, linked by shoulder bars, walked a cable five-eighths of an inch thick. Above them, two more men stood on the shoulder bars, and were themselves supporting a chair on shoulder bars. In the chair sat Karl Wallenda's niece.

"I can't hold any longer," shouted Karl's nephew as he walked the wire. It was his first performance with the troupe. Like a playing-card house, the pyramid at once collapsed. Karl and Herman clung safely to the wire, with Karl cradling his niece in his arms as he fastened his legs around the wire. But four of the men toppled 50 feet to the floor. Two were

Donna Farina (left) and Mia Wolff perform with the Big Apple Circus. (Carl Glassman)

killed, another was paralyzed permanently from the waist down, and a fourth was seriously injured.

The tragedy stunned the world, and there were attempts to make it illegal for acts like the Wallendas to perform without a net. Karl fought them. There were pleas from Helen to give it up before another family member died. Karl refused. The only death that could stop Karl Wallenda from performing would be his own, 18 years later.

Fearlessness may have been in the genes of the Wallendas or may come naturally to performers like Warren Bacon, but not all circus aerialists are instantly at home with great heights. Just a few months after her first climb to a tent-top perch in the Big Apple Circus, 26-year-old Mia Wolff vividly recalled the sickening queasiness in her stomach during those first work-outs.

"The body sends you signals that you're going to fall, you're going to panic, you're going to die," says Wolff, who decided to take to the air after leg injuries cut short her career as a circus tumbler. "What you have to do is override it, you have to control it. You just hold on and do it."

The first act called for Wolff to hang by her knees from a trapeze while holding her partner, Donna Farina, another beginner, by the wrists. Farina would swing her legs above her head as Wolff let go of her partner's wrists and grabbed her ankles. Although both women were tied to "mechanicals" (safety devices), Wolff was scared to release her partner.

"I wasn't afraid *I* was going to fall, I was afraid *she* would fall. What I finally had to do was let go on purpose, let her drop, and see that she wasn't going to fall to the ground."

As if the fear was not enough, there was also pain. Pressure of 220 pounds—the combined weight of the two women — would grind the back of Wolff's knees as she'd hang upside down, holding Donna. It took time and torture for that tender skin to turn a tough brown, giving her the padding she needed to make it through her act.

In the beginning, she would hang from the trapeze holding Farina while her trainer, Gregory Fedin, held a stopwatch, each day pushing her to bear the pain a few seconds longer. "You come to the point where you think you can't hold any longer and you hold it another five seconds and another five seconds."

Already, there are scars from her first few months as an aerialist. Two deep rope burns cut across her thigh and back, the results of a small miscalculation made while rope-sliding from her trapeze to the ground.

For Donna Farina, the challenge was to strengthen her small, delicate frame for high altitude acrobatics. Working low at first, she started gaining endurance simply by hanging from a trapeze. When even that 15-foot height was threatening, her trainer climbed onto a

Warren Bacon, along with partner Jessica Hentoff, makes aerial acrobatics look easy. (Carl Glassman)

chair so that Farina would be within reassuring reach. As with her partner, there was always the push beyond endurance. "I just couldn't grip anymore, but my trainer would still make me work," Farina recalls. "It was just pure torture and I thought, 'Oh, my God, I'll just never be strong enough.'" Slowly, calluses formed, and little by little Donna Farina got stronger.

Mia and Donna are still beginners in the world of flying. New tricks come slowly, and there are many shaky moments, but the most important ingredient to safety and success is already there: absolute mutual trust. When each one's life depends on the other, there is no room for doubt about a firm and fast grip or a perfectly timed catch. When Donna talks about their partnership, she reveals much about the conflicting qualities it takes to be daring—and remain alive.

"You put the two of us together and we balance each other out. Mia is more calm and always in control and I'm always excited and more—maybe—daring. If I were to do something crazy, she would be there to try and calm it down. And if she feels like she needs a push to get up and do something, I'll be there to push her."

Donna's tone dips into sadness when she's asked how her parents feel about what she does. "They're not too happy about it," she admits. "My mother is always having nightmares. My father is a little calmer.

"They saw our act once, when we were a lot

less experienced, and they were really scared. But they're going to come back again and I think they'll like it — just because we're a lot more secure now than we were then."

Donna tries not to think about the unpleasant side — her parents' fears, the pain, all the stories of accidents. And really, it isn't hard to forget, especially when she's floating and falling and spinning above a full house — all eyes fixed on her as solidly as the bright narrow beam of the spotlight.

"When the crowds are there and they love it," she says, her look now distant and dreamy, "I feel like I could just reach the ends of the world and do anything, anything, anything."

BOMB SQUAD

Wes Somerville is a gambler, of sorts. A man who stands to lose more than any Las Vegas crapshooter because the bet he stakes is his life. So far, Somerville, a 21-year veteran of the New York City Police Department's Bomb Squad, is a winner.

"You have to concentrate on the probability rather than the possibility," he says.

The "probability" is that when Somerville approaches a time bomb and gingerly attempts to disarm it, his expertise and experience will bring him through those harrowing moments alive. The "possibility" is that time will run out on the bomb as he walks toward it, or that he'll accidentally trigger any one of a number of booby traps that may lie in deadly wait of the slightest jar, tilt, or snip of the wrong wire. The odds may be with Somerville, but there are an awful lot of people who would say that he's crazy for taking them.

"We don't consider that our job is any more dangerous than a cop walking the beat," says the 58-year-old detective, who did just that for four years before joining the Bomb Squad. "If we have a bomb, we know there's a danger there. But the cop on the beat knows every day that something can happen, only he's not forewarned. He never knows whether some psycho is going to drive by in a car and shoot him."

Maybe so. But there are no long lines of patrolmen waiting to transfer into the Bomb Squad, even though it is one of the most prestigious sections of the police force—and even though in its 73-year history, the squad has suffered only four fatalities.

For the oldest and busiest bomb squad in the country (New York City has had as many as 10,000 bomb threats in a year) that's an astonishing record.

Originally, New York's Bomb Squad was called the Italian Squad, because its main job was to combat Italian hoodlums who used bombs to extort money from their newly immigrated compatriots. The squad's first leader, and its first victim, was Lt. Joseph Petrosino, who was shot in the back in Sicily while on a mission to exchange criminal intelligence with local officials.

Renamed the Alien Squad after World War I, the tiny group of about five men spent most of

Charlie Wells helps Ed Carney on with a protective bomb suit. The suit was developed by the British for use in bomb-torn Northern Ireland. (Carl Glassman)

its time matching wits with political terrorists who tried to create panic with a wave of bombings. During the late 1920s and early '30s, when its main job was combatting the explosives used by warring gangsters, the squad took on its present name.

It wasn't until 1940 that the squad lost men in a bomb blast. Two members approached a suspicious suitcase that had been lying for days in the World's Fair Irish Pavilion. Just as the men bent down to open it, the bomb inside exploded, killing them both.

The squad's archenemy for the next 16 years was a lunatic known only as "The Mad Bomber," a disgruntled employee of the local gas and electric company, who terrorized the city with pipe bombs. The police department beefed up the Bomb Squad's troops, adding Police Officer Wes Somerville. A few months later George "The Mad Bomber" Matesky was arrested and convicted.

Somerville, like most of those in the elite 12-man squad, had hands-on explosives experience in the military before becoming a policeman. As a bomb disposal specialist in the Army during World War II, he had disarmed unexploded bombs dropped by the Germans. Joining the Bomb Squad, however, meant that his education in explosives had just begun. Since the days of George Matesky, bombs have gotten more powerful and sophisticated. They are planted mostly by radical groups for one cause or another, and are often constructed by explosives experts. "The makeup of the device," says one Bomb Squad detective, "is only limited by the imagination of the bomb-maker." Which means if he's smart enough — and if he wants to badly enough — he can kill you. There are switches, for example, that set off the bomb if it's opened certain ways, jarred, picked up, or even x-rayed.

Keeping up with terrorist technology is a big step toward staying alive. New York's Bomb Squad hears about virtually every bomb that is planted around the world, and exchanges information with other police departments on the latest exploding devices — when the squads are lucky enough to find the bombs intact. Somerville downplays the danger, but he'll tell you that the worst moments come when facing a kind of device he's never seen before.

"If you can, don't be the first guy to get a new type of bomb," he says. "I had the first letter bomb that came into New York. After I opened and disarmed it, I saw how everything worked. I came back and everybody looked and got an idea of how it was put together. But the first one is a little... " and his voice trails off.

Each time one of the phones rings in the Bomb Squad office, there's a chance that *this* call will be that unwelcomed first, the one that might outsmart these experts. Then again it could be just routine business, or the press, or a call to investigate a bombing that just occurred. The atmosphere in the office is remarkably relaxed and never changes even when that phone rings. But if the caller says "suspicious package," within seconds a two-man team is out the door and on the way to the scene.

Chances are the call will not come from a civilian, but from the police department's Emergency Service, which is the first to be notified when a suspicious package is reported. Like paramedics who administer first aid while waiting for the doctor, the Emergency Service is trained to identify what could be a life-threatening situation. If they think there's a chance it's the real thing they will usually cover the object with a styrofoam picnic basket and place over that a "bomb blanket," constructed of nylon ballistic cloth. If the bomb explodes before the squad arrives, the shrapnel will at least partly be contained within the blanket, which puffs up like a parachute on impact, then settles back down.

"When I arrive at the scene, and as I'm walking up to the thing," Somerville says, "Emergency Service gives me pertinent information about the device, even before I ask the questions. So my mind is eliminating certain possibilities and retaining others. For example, some bombs have anti-disturbance switches. So the first thing I want to know is how did the package get there. If the mailman brought it or the custodian found it downstairs and he put it in his room, I know somebody's been moving this thing. Now the chances are I can move it.

It's no guarantee, because there are bombs that can be moved once, set down, and then the next guy that moves it...But you can't worry about everything.

"If the package hasn't been moved," says Somerville, "the first thing I do is move it. I put a rope around it, get the hell back, and give it a tug."

When high-level government officials come to town, members of the Bomb Squad, along with a dog and dog handler, stay one step ahead of them at all times. The dog is trained to sit beside a package in which he smells an explosive. "Then," says Somerville, "we pet him and love him and get him the hell out of the room. Then I start working on the package."

Just exactly how Bomb Squad men enter packages is something they don't like to describe in too much detail. ("We're paranoid," says Somerville.) But one golden rule is always observed: Never open the container the way it was intended.

The squad has a number of tools to help give them a picture of what's inside the package without opening it. Listening devices, fluoroscopes, or portable X-ray machines may be used. But, because the men literally work against the clock, they don't really like anything that could slow them up. "You don't use the tools under every condition," says Somerville. "It's almost like a sixth sense that tells you when you have time to use them and when you don't. Besides," he adds, "the pictures

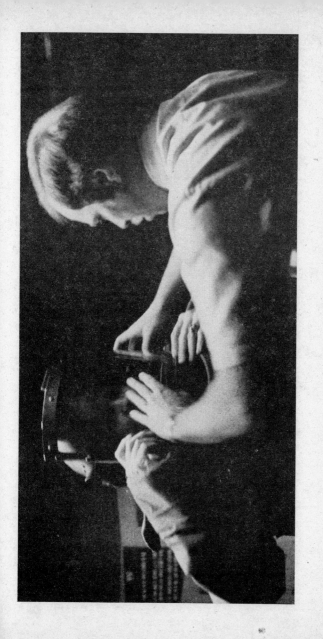

you sometimes get from a fluoroscope can scare the hell out of you. There are so many things that people carry, like a travel alarm or an electric razor with a wire. I see the clockwork and the wires and right away I'm saying, 'Oh, boy, what have I got here?'"

The job that stands out most vividly in Somerville's mind was no false alarm.

"I got a call that they had found an attaché case on a 19th-floor fire escape of a Russian importing company. I got over there and as I'm going up in the elevator the cop who's bringing me up says, 'Boy, that was some blast.' I said, 'What blast?' and he told me that the thing had gone off. Just as I get to the 19th floor and begin looking through the hole in the floor to the 18th floor, trying to figure out what went off, someone says, 'Hey, we've got another one right above.' I tell everyone to get the hell out and the guy takes me up and shows me another attaché case."

As soon as he'd cut an inspection hole, Somerville knew that "this isn't what you carry every day in your briefcase." Not quite. What he found were four sticks of dynamite wired to a ticking kitchen timer. Two seconds after he disarmed the bomb the clock struck zero and a small light inside a file-card case (installed by the bomb maker to test the electrical circuit) flashed on—"scaring the living daylights out of me."

Somerville claims he wasn't frightened while he was working on the device. "You're much too busy," he says. "You're thinking of everything." Instead, fear, like a bomb, has its own delayed reaction. A month after his brush with death, he recalls, "I was working alone and I got a call at about two o'clock in the morning about a suspected bomb. As I'm driving to the scene I say, 'Hey, I'm out of my mind. I could get hurt on this job.' And then I started to get a little bit scared."

Why does he take the chances, then? He's no daredevil. "It's like climbing a mountain. Why do you climb a mountain? Because it's there, right? You couldn't get me up there. My daughter goes out with a guy who's a parachute jumper, and he wants to take me. I say you need a whip and a chair to get me out of that plane."

To hear him talk, you'd think that Somerville has just the average guy's taste for adventure. "I think everybody finds something to add a little excitement to his life," he says. "Hell, we cross in between and not on the green. You run across Sixth Avenue for that cab. You're not supposed to do it. You know all the things that could happen to you, but you do it anyway."

For the five years he served in the New York City Police Department's Bomb Squad, Officer Brian Murray also knew the dangers involved. But, like his colleagues, he trusted self-confidence, experience, and a touch of luck to see him through. "He always told me, 'Don't worry, I never take any chances,' " Murray's wife, Kathleen, related to *The New York Times* reporter Roy Silver. " 'I have a wife and two children to take care of.' " But Kathleen wasn't convinced. She had persuaded her husband to apply for a transfer out of the Bomb Squad—in fact, the papers had already been filed—when he was killed in 1976.

The fatal explosion was not in Grand Central Station, where Murray had just helped remove the bomb from a locker and load it onto the bomb truck. Instead, he died in the controlled "safety" of Rodman's Neck, the police firing range where the bombs are taken to be detonated. For 15 minutes, Murray and three other Bomb Squad members tried unsuccessfully to blow up the bomb by remote control. The four of them then approached the device in the demolition pit and it went off, killing Murray and injuring the other three men.

It was the first Bomb Squad death since 1940. The tragedy shook the other men and their families, making them more painfully aware of the dangerous realities of the job. When Somerville's son, a fireman, heard on the radio that a Bomb Squad man was killed and others were injured, he called the police department in tears trying to find out if his father was among them. Somerville's wife urged him to quit. And the day after the tragedy, a member of the squad opened a suspicious package wearing a protective vest for the first time in 20 years.

Nevertheless, the men do not question their

A lone bomb-squad man works against the clock as he disarms a device outside a New York City court house. (N.Y. *Daily News*)

commitment to the squad, lest they tamper with their own self-confidence. Somerville says quitting never entered his mind. Even as they investigated the explosion that killed their comrade, they treated it as they would any other bombing probe. "It was another explosion," says Somerville. "We had a fatality and people injured — except that they were our own."

Almost two years after Murray's death, in August, 1978, Police Officer Edward Carney found himself speeding toward Manhattan's Grand Central Station at four o'clock in the morning. In a locker, near the one that had contained the device that killed Brian Murray, a bomb waited for him. It had been planted by Croatian terrorists, the same group responsible for Murray's death. All this flashed through Carney's mind as his siren broke the quiet of a nearly deserted Forty-second Street. He had just wound up a tense early-morning job and now it looked like he was beginning another.

Half an hour earlier, Carney and his partner, Arthur Hornidge, were in the office when the phone rang. Emergency Service reported a suspicious package at the United Nations. What they found resting on a window ledge of the U.N. library was a Heineken six-pack container. Instead of beer, the package contained five sticks of dynamite, a blasting cap, and an electrical mechanism. On the outside of the package was an alarm clock and a pipe, sealed at both ends.

Had the device worked properly, it would have exploded by the time the men arrived. But this was a dreaded "hang fire." The hand of the clock didn't quite make sufficient contact to complete the electrical circuit and explode the dynamite.

The pipe, which they feared contained a separate bomb, instead held a communiqué from the terrorists. A U.N. guard recognized the language as Croatian.

Carney wrapped the bomb in a bomb blanket and gingerly carried it to the bomb truck, a specially protected vehicle designed for transporting explosives back to Rodman's Neck. As Carney walked away feeling the relief and satisfaction of a job well done, a lieutenant approached with more news. "Hey, did you guys hear? They have another device at Grand Central."

Most suspicious packages turn out to be harmless. But this time Carney knew before he ever reached the train station that this was a bomb. When he arrived, Carney saw the men from Emergency Service drilling a hole into the side of the locker. "Whoa, this could be the real thing," he called to them. "Stop what you're doing right away." Carney peeked through the hole and saw another Heineken's package. "Here we go again," he thought to himself. Making sure the door latch wasn't booby-trapped, he opened the locker and went to work in the confined space of the small compartment. Once again, Carney successfully dismantled the device, and once again he called for the bomb truck. It was finally the end to a long morning, one he's not likely to forget.

"Every time I see a six pack of Heineken," Carney says, "it gives me nightmares."

The United Nations, like Grand Central Station, has been the target of terrorists more than once. On a January morning in 1976, three alarm clocks ticked away inside a shopping bag in an underground passageway while, upstairs, members of the U.N. Security Council readied for a fierce debate on the Mideast. A cleaning person, making his rounds through the tunnel, discovered the bag and peered inside. What he saw was a black airline-type tote bag with wires and a battery sticking out.

Minutes later, at 11:30 a.m., the phone rang in the Bomb Squad office. The moment that Detectives Charles Wells and Bill Schmitt heard where the bag was found, they knew this was no false alarm. The information over the phone was sketchy, but Wells and Schmitt were already discussing possible plans of attacking the device even as they dashed to their car.

When they arrived at the U.N., the police had evacuated the buildings and cleared the street. It was just Wells and Schmitt alone, walking the 30 yards from their car to the package. Eyeballing the paperbag all the way, they felt good that they first had only the bag to enter. It, at least, could not be booby-trapped.

The men took from their pockets two small leather cases full of cutting tools, and opened the bag from the side. Inside were two airline bags and a plastic garbage bag. Wells and Schmitt decided not to test for anti-disturbance switches, usually done by standing at a safe distance and tugging on the bags with twine. It was a personal decision and other men might have done it differently. "If it has an anti-disturbance switch it's going to go off," Wells figured, "which is exactly what the perpetrator wanted in the first place. By moving the package without testing it first, it's not that you hope it's not an anti-disturbance device, but you feel you can beat it if it is."

Wells and Schmitt placed the three bags 15 feet apart, far enough that if one went off it wouldn't trigger the other two. Working together on the first black bag, they cut an inspection hole in the side and saw a pipe, a battery, and a spaghetti-like confusion of twisted wires. Then they cut the hole still larger, and saw before them a ticking clock. Now they knew they had a live device. What they didn't know was how much time was left to dismantle it. The face of the clock was masked with tape. To peel off the tape would mean wasting precious seconds that could separate life from death. And disturbing the two wires leading to the clock could also mean disaster.

Wells and Schmitt, however, were not just working against time. The wiring of the device was like a miniature minefield. At three points in the circuit the wires were bare, separated by a mere eighth of an inch. The slightest movement could have made the wires touch and the bomb explode. Also, the two wires were running through the same piece of plastic insulation. If they cut at the wrong point in the circuit through both wires, the metal cutters would have completed the circuit, detonating the bomb. There was the chance, too, that cutting only one wire would not have disarmed the bomb, but merely collapsed the circuit and detonated it. "You come to a point," says Wells, "where you have to take a chance one way or another."

Before the men did any cutting, they had to remove a propane tank that was securely taped to the pipe. The terrorists had included the fuel to create a giant fireball when the bomb exploded and set part of the U.N. in flames.

With surgical precision they cut correctly, separating the explosives from the power source.

While working on the bomb, Wells was too busy analyzing the circuitry to be nervous. But as he rushed to the next black zippered bag, he wondered how much time was left. A couple of hours — or a couple of ticks. "The only way I'm going to go," Wells always said, "is if the time just happens to run out when I'm walking up to it."

Time didn't run out and the second black bag posed no problem. It was the same circuitry as the first.

After disarming a bomb at a Russian import-export company, Wes Somerville carries it onto a specially protected truck. If Somerville had been two seconds later, he would have been killed. (N.Y. *Daily News*)

Next they faced the plastic garbage bag. The men didn't expect to find a bomb here too, but they quickly proved themselves wrong. Another clock ticked away. More wires were cut.

In 10 minutes, from the time the team arrived to the last snip, it was over. Almost. The men still had on their hands three sealed pipes. They felt sure the explosives had been rendered safe. But there was the chance that inside the pipes was more circuitry—a terrorist's second chance. Wells put on a protective vest, wrapped the pipes in bomb blankets, and put them in special baskets. A pole was slipped through the handle of the basket, then each man took an end of the pole and carried the explosives like big-game hunters toting their bounty.

Once back at the firing range, the trick was to uncap the pipe with a special explosive, without detonating the dynamite — thereby salvaging evidence for a possible court case. The first time, it didn't work.

Wells was 300 feet from the bomb, ducking behind a car, when it exploded. Shrapnel from the pipe and the woven steel basket that held it sailed overhead for another 100 feet past him. "Watching it go off gave me a good feeling, a feeling of relief that it didn't go off while I was next to it. But it made me a little queasy, too, to see that steel fly 400 feet."

Wells spent that evening watching himself on TV, switching from one news show to the next. Relatives called from across the country to congratulate him. And later, he was awarded an Honorable Mention ribbon, the police department's highest award.

"When the call comes in that there's a suspicious package or a ticking package," says Wells, "I don't really hope it's a bomb. But when it is — and after I've disarmed it, I feel good, I feel high. It's the same as when I was in uniform and I took a gun off somebody."

Those "highs" are earned mostly by skill and experience. But Wells admits that there's one more important factor. "The way I look at it," he says, "if you're competent, if you've got the knowledge, then that's at least 50 percent of it. But it's just luck, too, I guess, that it doesn't make its final tick when you're next to it."

RACE-CAR
DRIVER

Formula road racing has been called the world's most dangerous sport, and Bobby Rahall is considered one of racing's most promising young American drivers. Whether or not he's the next Mario Andretti, an American Grand Prix world champion, his rise so far has been impressive. On his way up, Rahall sharpened his skills in the U.S. and Canada with Formula Atlantic competitions, the training ground for American Formula One drivers, and Formula Three in Europe. In 1978, at the age of 25, he earned a ride in two Formula One Grand Prix races.

It's not surprising that Rahall steered his life in the direction of road racing. With a father who raced Porsches and Lotuses for a hobby, Rahall has been going to races since the age of four. By junior high school he was working for his father as a mechanic and helper, and at 17 drove his first race car.

By the time he finished college in 1975, Rahall had put aside his plans for a career in law and taken to the road full-time. Like many drivers who enter this extremely expensive sport, Rahall comes from a wealthy family. His father's financial backing put him on the circuit for two years, but it was his own skill that kept him there. In 1976, after an outstanding first season as a professional, Rahall caught the eye of a sponsor, who financed him for the next two years. In 1979, after narrowly missing a chance for Formula One sponsorship, Rahall raced through Europe's Formula Two circuits.

Here, Bobby Rahall talks about his dangerous and exciting life.

What attracts you to racing?

The speed. It's tremendously exciting. Also, making a car do something that very few people can do. I couldn't convey what driving a racing car is like because there's something magical about it. You're off by yourself and it's just you and this piece of machinery. What you do with it is up to you. You're in a very responsible position, too. People work hours upon hours upon hours giving you the chance to go out and do your thing. You want to reward them, to do a good job for the mechanics and the rest of the team.

What about the glamour?

It's there. There's the jet set and the beautiful people and so forth. But for the drivers and the mechanics there's a lot of work. We're not going to dinner with Princess Grace every night. Half the time you're testing in the middle of nowhere and it's cold and raining and you forgot to bring your sweater. Sometimes it's so lonely that you want to shoot yourself.

What makes a good race-car driver?

More than anything, you need to have a desire to be a success—to be the best and to do something that very few people can do. You also need to be an optimist and believe there really is a pot of gold at the end of the rainbow, because generally the disappointments are greater than the victories.

In terms of natural abilities, you have to have a good sense of balance. There's a very thin line between being in control and being out of control. It's a tightrope walk and you're walking it all the time.

It used to be said that you couldn't be a Grand Prix driver if you wore glasses. But being successful as a driver or a pilot or anything that has to do with hand-eye coordination is not so much determined by how good your eyes are. What's important is how good your eyes are at interpreting what they're seeing, and how quickly it goes from your brain to your hands or to your feet. Because of the speeds you're traveling, distances close up quick—260 feet per second. Sometimes, if there's an accident up ahead, you're going to be involved in it no matter what you do. But many times a good driver can avoid it if his thinking is a reflex

Bobby Rahall on the job...(Marc Spraule)

...and at home. (Carl Glassman)

instead of a process. If a car up ahead has started to spin, a good driver immediately chooses to move left, say, instead of thinking indecisively right-left-right-left. You have to make a decision and stick with it.

How do you stay calm?

If you're tense you just burn up energy and you're fighting the car all the time. Relaxing allows you to almost melt into the car. You can go far longer at far greater speeds. Even though you're going very quickly, everything is in order. Everything happens slowly in your mind. That only comes from racing a lot.

How do they make seats that are perfectly comfortable for each driver?

They seat you in a big plastic garbage bag, then pour this foam down the back. It creates a molding of your body.

Is physical strength important?

People don't realize it, but it takes a great deal of strength to hold a 1400-pound car through a 150-mile-an-hour corner. The faster you go around a corner the greater the force is taking it away from the corner. Your chest, back, and forearm muscles get very built up because those are the ones you use to keep the car in control. Let's say you drove an ordinary car in a big circle and drove it around as fast as you could until the tires couldn't hold it on the road any longer. Up to that point the most gravitational force pulling you would be 1½ g's (50 percent more than normal). In a Formula

One racing car you pull 2½ g's. Your head, which weighs 10 pounds normally, now weighs 25 pounds. So holding your head in with a helmet takes a great deal of strength in the neck. And keeping the car in control requires strength.

Do you think race-car drivers are especially courageous?

Most people, if they saw me on the racetrack, might think I was either crazy or extremely brave, but I don't think of myself as being brave. If you don't romanticize what you're doing, you see racing more as a technological feat than a test of daring. You might go through a corner 10 miles an hour faster than everybody else, but really you're just doing what you already know you can do with that car. In fact, it's probably braver to drive a car that doesn't handle well and be going slower. Because when a car doesn't handle, you're fighting it and you're on the edge of disaster all the time.

Isn't there a certain thrill to, say, taking a corner a little faster than you think you should, and getting away with it?

I think that's Hollywood. Hollywood's got it in everybody's mind that it's a thrill to cheat death. But if you talk to most drivers I think you'll find that very few of them are in it for that.

As race cars become faster, does racing get more dangerous?

68

Just the opposite. The cars have become much safer, the circuits are safer, and protection for the driver just in the last 10 years has leaped a thousandfold. For example, being trapped in your car when it catches on fire used to be one of the most feared things in racing. Ten years ago you had maybe a second to get out of your car before it went up in flames. Now you have about a minute and a half. It's like the Stone Age versus the Renaissance.

How does your suit protect you from the flames?

The suit itself is made of fire-retardant material. And in the helmet I have a tube that comes out the side and is hooked up to what they call a "life support system." In the event of fire you push the fire button and a heavier-than-air atmosphere comes through the helmet and keeps fire from getting in. Most fire deaths are not caused by the burns but by inhaling heat, which sears the lungs.

What brought on the improved safety in racing?

Unfortunately, changes only happen after someone gets hurt. Like airplane disasters, until the event happens no one does much about it. In the mid-1960s a fair number of drivers were killed. I think out of all that came a great desire to make racing safer. You can still get killed or injured, but the number of fatalities is much fewer than what it was even eight or nine years ago.

Since Formula One races are the fastest, are they also the most dangerous?

Formula One circuits and cars are tremendously safe compared to those you experience on your way up. You're going at greater speeds, to be sure, but I think the chances of major injury are greater in the lower formulas. For one thing, in the lower formulas, cars are not prepared correctly because cost is a factor. Instead of going out and spending $500 for a good fire system, the owner would rather save the money. Then the car crashes and burns. Or he'll spend $80 for a driver's suit instead of $300 and there's going to be a difference in the way you're protected.

When it comes to safety, is there much difference between Grand Prix drivers and those who are on their way up?

People take more chance in the lower formulas. They really want Formula One, so valor becomes the better part of discretion instead of the other way around, and that's when you get into accidents. You have people trying to fit four cars in where only three can go and sooner or later something's going to happen. Very few people get killed, but there are a lot of broken legs, broken arms, things like that.

Do you worry about getting killed?

It's trite to say it, but life is terminal. I mean, no one wants to die. I don't have a death-wish. I want to be old and gray and have grandchildren. But by confronting the possibility of death so often, maybe it makes you better prepared for the consequences. Maybe because we're prepared to die, we appreciate things a little bit more. Maybe we drivers feel that the quality of life is better than the quantity.

What worries you the most when you're racing?

I know that I won't make such a bad mistake that I'll get hurt. When drivers get hurt it's when things break. A tire goes flat all of a sudden or a suspension piece breaks. At the speeds you're traveling you have no control. The car just sort of finds its own path. You're effectively a passenger at that point.

Has that happened to you?

I've had some fairly wild rides, but luckily I haven't been hurt. At the track in Limerock, Connecticut, there's a corner onto the straightaway that's very fast — it's fifth gear and just flat out. It comes down a hill and bends around and there's a big earth bank 20 or 30 feet off the side of the circuit. During practice, the day before the race, I was at the bottom of that hill, just starting the turn at 140 miles an hour. The outside front tire deflated suddenly and the car just went straight and I think the only words I said to myself were, "Damn, this is going to hurt" and boom, I hit, and nothing happened. I couldn't believe it. I hit a big wall of tires tied together that cushioned the impact. What really surprised me was that there was very little damage to the car. In fact, I won the race the next day.

Can you do anything to protect yourself in a situation like that?

Driver Joe Frasson narrowly escapes from his burning car during a 1979 race at the Daytona International Speedway in Florida. Frasson was unhurt. (Wide World Photos)

You really have so little time. All you do is brace yourself, duck your head, and pull your arms in.

What goes through your mind when you pass an accident?

I was in one race where a guy was badly hurt. I went by that wreck and I said "Boy, that looks bad." But I saw him in the car and he was moving. You have to be an optimist and figure the guy got away with it. Maybe it shows how divorced you have to be from emotion to drive a racing car, but when you see an accident you don't think anything of it.

Nothing?

Certainly no one is so cold-blooded that seeing a guy on fire they're going to say to themselves, "Tough luck, Charlie." But by the same token you've got a job to do. If you start thinking about that you'd better get out of the car, because it's going to happen to you.

High-speed racing in the rain looks impossibly dangerous. What's it like from the driver's seat?

The slightest mistake becomes a major error. I was in a race this year in which I couldn't see 10 feet ahead of me. There was so much water coming down that you were just blind. It's just gray in front of you. You have to keep your foot on the gas because otherwise you might get run over. All you can do is look to the side of the road, hoping to recognize something that will tell you when to turn.

Do some drivers try to settle grudges on the track by knocking opponents off the circuit?

You don't purposely go out and hit somebody, but sometimes it happens. Sometimes you have a disagreement over who should be where, when. Accidents happen. But I don't think there's anybody who seriously goes out and says, "I'm going to knock you off the circuit."

What do you consider the most exciting part of the race?

There is nothing more spectacular than a Formula One start. Everyone goes off on a pace lap very slowly until you're lined up on a dummy grid, with everybody in the proper order. Then they hang up a 20-second board and the cars roll up to the main grid very slowly, then stop. The crescendo starts to build and the engines get louder and louder to a feverish pitch. Everything is up — and they go.

Invariably, the first turn is where the accidents happen. Adrenaline is running high, the tires and brakes are cold, and you're bunched up close together. If you get past that, you're usually in good shape for the rest of the race.

With all the money and attention spent on these cars, why do they still break down?

Because they're like jet fighters. You're trying to make them as light as they can possibly be and yet as strong. But unlike a fighter, racing cars don't have the room for a back-up system. It's a piece of machinery that is highly

74

Crashes frequently occur at the beginning of a Grand Prix race, when drivers scramble to break ahead of the pack. In this start of the 1978 British Grand Prix, America's Mario Andretti is in front. But the winding race was won by Carlos Reutemann of Argentina.

stressed and, unfortunately, it happens to break down.

In jet planes, certain parts are automatically replaced after flying a prescribed number of hours. Isn't that also true of racing cars?

The car that starts the season is never the same car that finishes. It's the same chassis and number, but otherwise it's probably been replaced two or three times during the year. Parts that may have been good for four races are replaced after only two. But you're still dealing with a piece of machinery under high stress. It's very light and very fragile. If you bully the gearbox, if you start mashing gears a little bit too soon or late, it will break down.

What are your future goals as a driver?

Becoming world champion. That will serve to provide me and my family, through our endorsements, a certain amount of freedom and leisure in our lives. I hope to be able to work it so that I can be successful quickly and retire at 31 or 32.

Why quit so young?

Racing's a job, that's all it is. It's exciting, but eight or ten years of traveling every weekend can become tiring. And let's not lose sight of the fact that the longer you race, the greater the chance of something happening. There's still that risk.

DECOYS

The street is dark and the doorway, a rear theater exit, is even darker. About the only signs of life on this New York City street are the shadowy forms of a few pedestrians and an old lady slumped down at the theater door.

Despite the darkness the woman wears huge sunglasses. And despite the warmth of the night, two kerchiefs are wrapped around her blond hair. Beneath her light-blue housedress she's wearing still more layers of clothing, including long pants and a shirt.

Like so many other "shopping bag ladies" who live in the streets of large cities, all her worldly possessions seem to be nestled beside her. With one hand, the woman loosely holds the handle of a large plastic bag, filled with a camera, coin purse, Kentucky Fried Chicken box, and other assorted treasures buried beneath. In the other hand, hidden inside the pocket of her Salvation Army dress, she fingers a .38 caliber revolver.

The woman is Maureen DeStasio, an 11-year veteran of the New York City Police Department, who has served for the last six years as a police decoy. Her job: to get mugged. As she feigns sleep, her head bent down to hide the features of an attractive and youthful-looking 38-year-old, her eyes are secretly fixed on the shopping bag bait, and her ears remain attuned to the voices and footsteps of approaching muggers lured by a "helpless" lady's possessions.

While DeStasio watches the loot, other policemen, from a garage across the street, watch her. The two men slouching down inside the red Chevy are plainclothesmen, their eyes peeled, ready to take off if the mugger runs. And down at the corner, the young bearded guy who seems to be talking on the phone is also a policeman prepared to cut off the suspect if he tries to escape the other way.

In the meantime, DeStasio sits and waits. For hours at a time, in warm weather and in cold, she remains almost motionless. Occasionally she pulls out of her bag a long strip of toilet paper to blow her nose, or slightly repositions her body against the hard concrete steps, or, most important, taps her head.

It's that head tap that the other officers are waiting for. That's the signal that property has been taken and it's time to move in for an

In a Times Square garage, Police decoy Maureen De-Stasio and a colleague prepare for a night's work on the streets. (Carl Glassman)

arrest. If all goes well, the mugger will be apprehended and whisked to the back of an unmarked car without ever learning that his intended victim was part of a trap. And if all goes well, no harm comes to DeStasio.

In six years and 250 muggings, all *has* gone well. But there is always the possibility of danger. In her defenseless pose, DeStasio is an easy mark for a mugger bent on violence.

Most nights DeStasio and her team of backups (she rotates among some eight teams in her squad) work in the Times Square area, a neighborhood that houses both legitimate theaters and pornographic movie houses, bars, and other signs of seedy night life. The area, says DeStasio, attracts more than its share of undesirables and as a woman she is especially vulnerable to abuse—regardless of how badly she's dressed or how old she looks.

On one occasion, DeStasio recalls, "Two guys in their twenties pulled up in front of me in a car. One of them comes over to me and says, 'Where do you live, I'll take you home.' I said 'No, I'm waiting for my sister.' I thought the guy was going to take my wallet or something. Instead he said to me, 'We're the police, you have to come with us,' and he shows me a fake badge. Now I know I have a collar [an arrest for criminal impersonation of a police officer] right off the bat, but I wanted to see if he'd do more. I refused to go with him so he dragged me off the steps. Then his partner got out and the two of them tried to drag me into the car—at which point I drew my gun on them. I wasn't going in anybody's car." The two men jumped into the car and tried to escape from the scene, but were apprehended by the back-up cops. It is perhaps the greatest satisfaction of her job that, for at least a night, she saves someone else from becoming a victim of something even more serious than thievery.

"I really don't like anyone to touch me," says DeStasio, who is subject to strangers shaking her to see if she's awake, searching her for money, or worse. "But sometimes someone will grab me, and then I just tap my head, or on occasion I've as much as punched a guy in the face. I'm not going to sit there and be abused. That's not what we're there for, but unfortunately in this area it happens a lot."

DeStasio emphasizes that the decoy routine is practiced as safely as possible, and downplays the dangers. Still, she admits, "Anytime you can meet up with a nut who just wants to hurt you."

There was, for example, the "psycho" who walked past her, dressed in a long robe over his pants, and began beating her with a stick. The man was quickly apprehended and DeStasio wasn't badly hurt.

Strangely enough, the two times she was actually injured on the job were both the results of blows from other police officers. During New York City's 1977 blackout, dressed as always in civilian clothes except for her police helmet, she was helping control a crowd of looters.

DeStasio went to retrieve another policeman's nightstick thrown at one of the looters—before it got in the wrong hands. "I bent over to pick it up and a uniformed sergeant came by and whacked me with his nightstick so hard," she recalls with a smile. "He didn't know I was a cop. He thought I was one of the bad guys. When I stood up he said, 'Oh, you're on the job.' I wore a bruise for two weeks."

The other injury came during decoy work, when she was dressed normally and sitting one night on a bench near an entrance to Central Park. After observing DeStasio for some time, two men approached her, one with his hand in his pocket, claiming to have a gun pointed at her. He told DeStasio to come into the park with them. "I got off the bench, but I was sure he didn't have a gun. I figured if they had a gun, why would it have taken them half an hour to get the nerve to come over. I had a shoulder holster on and I had my hand on my gun. I started walking with them as they were pulling me along. When I got to the park entrance I wasn't going any farther."

But when the back-up team moved in to make an arrest, the two men resisted and fists started to fly. One of them — coming from another cop — landed accidentally on the mouth of Maureen DeStasio. Fortunately, the worst she had to show for the episode was a fat lip and some embarrassment, but the episode proved that the decoy is far from immune to violence.

Still, DeStasio insists she's usually not afraid. Even her family gives little thought to the dangers of the job. "They're used to it now, I've been doing it for so long. In the beginning they were a little worried, but they're not anymore. Sometimes, when I leave, they'll say to be careful. I tell them it's not at all as dangerous as people think it is because I don't resist. I just let them take whatever they're going to take and then let the back-ups get them."

DeStasio does sometimes have "ominous feelings." There was the time, for example, when a rowdy gang stood by her as she sat in her usual, dark Times Square doorway. This time, however, empty wine bottles lay strewn around her. As she listened to the boys discuss whether she might be a decoy, DeStasio had visions of one of them breaking a bottle over her head. If that was about to happen, her back-ups down the street could never have saved her. DeStasio's fears passed only after the boys wandered away. (Months later, near the same spot, one of her colleagues was less fortunate. A mugger slashed the decoy's throat, almost killing him.)

"The time I *really* should have been afraid I wasn't. It came when I was serving as a rape decoy in Brooklyn. The man we were trying to catch had been grabbing women from behind and forcing them into doorways or onto rooftops. He also had a gun."

DeStasio recalls that on one of those nights

she had been followed by three boys as she walked along the street, but nothing happened. The next night the same trio followed her. Just before she was certain they would take her purse, a man from across the street approached her and pulled what at first appeared to be a gun.

"He said, 'Give me your pocketbook. I want all your money or I'm going to kill ya.' That's a time I should have been afraid. But I looked down and saw this gun that didn't even have a hole in it — I mean, my son had better guns when he was little. It was all I could do to keep from laughing at him. The sorry part of it was that when the back-ups saw him pull a gun, they jumped out of their car and ran right over. One of them yelled, 'Get out of the way, get out of the way!' I yelled back, 'Don't shoot him, don't shoot him, it's a fake gun!' He could have gotten shot because in a case like that, if I don't shoot the perpetrator, the back-ups should."

Decoy work rarely results in "gun collars" (arresting someone with a gun) but many of the would-be bandits carry knives — and very long arrest records. Getting them off the streets — even though their stays in jail are short — is important, says DeStasio, because many of them don't stop after stealing a wallet, a purse, or a camera. "If they have the opportunity, in doorways, hallways, and elevators, they can kill you easily."

Mostly, though, they just grab what they can

and run. Sometimes, two or three thieves who don't even know each other are apprehended at once. Two of them may be strolling by the decoy at the same time, get the same idea, and decide to divvy up the spoils. Or, after one guy gets his take, another thief mugs the mugger. Either way, they both end up in jail.

Usually, DeStasio waits for the robber to walk away before she taps her head, but sometimes she has to stop the crime sooner. "One guy was really ridiculous," she recalls. "He took everything I had. First he took the suitcase I was leaning against and he put it behind him. Then he took my bag and put it to the side. Since my pocketbook was over my arm, he just went through it and took out my wallet and a camera. After that I tapped my head. I figured this guy's going to go for my socks next."

Then there are the more scheming robbers. DeStasio remembers one man who grabbed her arm as she seemed to wander aimlessly along the sidewalk. "He said to me, 'Come on, you need a cup of coffee.' He took me into a coffee shop and ordered me a coffee. Then he reaches into my pocketbook, takes out *my* wallet, pays the guy for the coffee with his money, and walks out of the shop with my money."

At the age of 22, with a husband and two small children, Maureen DeStasio decided to become a policewoman. She is not quite sure what attracted her to the job ("I just walked into a precinct and asked how to go about becoming a cop") but after finally being accepted after four years of waiting, she was disappointed. In those days policewomen rarely did more than search female prisoners or type and file.

"I thought I would be doing police work," she recalls, still obviously bitter about her first years on the force. "When I was assigned matron duty I hated it and was very discouraged. I kind of thought I was being paid for more than I was doing." But the job only got worse when she was given clerical duties. Fortunately for her, in 1973 women became a more integral part of the police force, patrolling the streets, responding to emergencies, and doing most of the same work as men. It was about then that DeStasio had her worst experience since becoming a policewoman. She got mugged.

Going back to her car in a bad section of Brooklyn one day, she heard someone walking behind her. The approaching footsteps sounded like the clacking of high heels, so DeStasio didn't turn around. She should have. Following her was a six-foot-two male. "He grabbed my pocketbook. I held it. We fought for it and he won." Losing her purse — with service revolver inside—was especially painful and embarrassing because it made her realize that after so many years on the force she was still not street-wise.

As a result, DeStasio applied for the elite Street Crime Unit and was overjoyed to get it. "I thought to myself, now I'm going to get that guy."

DeStasio ambles towards her sidewalk "home," where she'll sit for hours in hopes of attracting muggers. (Carl Glassman)

Being a member of that unit has included much more than just decoy work. Much of the time is spent patrolling the streets of some of the city's most dangerous neighborhoods. Inside the cab or unmarked cruiser of each two- or three-person team, the mood is relaxed. With some Country-Western music twanging on the radio, the cops might be quietly singing, or discussing last night's Yankee game or an upcoming fishing trip. But their eyes are always watching, ever alert to a suspicious bulge in a coat, or an old woman being followed, or maybe a man hailing a cab with two of his friends obscured in a nearby darkened doorway.

More than half the time, says DeStasio, their suspicions prove correct. "You get a knack for knowing who the bad guys are. It's like they don't have a direction. They're looking around and moping around, they're plotting and planning, and looking at pocketbooks. You can just tell that they're up to no good."

In the policeman's world, gun collars usually are the "choice" arrests, the most prestigious, exciting, and dangerous. But after years in the shadows, dressed in the rags of the shopping bag lady, DeStasio has cultivated a special feeling for those defenseless women.

Riding out to an assignment one evening, DeStasio and her colleagues were kidding and joking as usual. Then the mood suddenly sobered. She mentioned a recent incident in one of the subway stations in which two boys, one of them nine and the other fifteen, were charged with setting a shopping bag lady afire. In the dead seriousness of very few words, De-Stasio summed up the essence of her work.

"I wish it'd been me they tried that on," she said. "I wish it'd been me."

Not every decoy dressed as a shopping bag lady is a lady. All men accepted into the elite Street Crime Unit must be willing to shave their beards, don dresses and wigs, and take to the streets, pocketbooks in hands, as easily muggable targets. As it turns out, only a few of the men have much success in the role.

Officer Gary Besmer is one of the best. People who know Besmer like to recall the night his team was breaking in a new female decoy. For hours the woman sat on a dimly lit street without so much as a nibble from a passing mugger. Finally, Besmer decided to show the rookie how it was done. He rolled up the legs of his pants, put on his bulky woman's coat and wig and took her place. Within minutes the team had made an arrest. Quite a feat, considering Besmer was wearing a mustache. Even the thief told him he deserved an Academy Award.

Besmer has since shaved off his mustache. But he only masquerades as a woman in colder weather because the heavy coat is an essential part of his disguise. When he does do the decoy routine, it's far safer than when he started. "The muggers used to grab your watch and it was like a natural reflex to grab the guy. It took us six months to a year to learn to let the back-up team do everything."

Besmer's most harrowing experience as a decoy came when a mugger did, in fact, try to take his watch. Instead of dressing as an old lady, his left arm was in a fake cast to make him appear helpless — and for a critical moment that's exactly what he was. "I jumped up and grabbed him, but I couldn't get my arm out of the cast. I was trying to hold onto him with my right arm, waiting for the back-up to move in. I told him I was a police officer but he started punching. And he kept on beating, beating. We got him, but we couldn't figure out why he was resisting. As it turned out, he had escaped from Maryland, where he was serving a life plus two for murder and rape. He had a lot to lose and if he had had a weapon he would have used it. He couldn't go back to jail for any longer if he killed me."

Besmer's two partners — and his back-ups when he's a decoy — are Jerry Rice and Dan Bronte. Together, the trio is known in the Street Crime Unit as the Munchkins, because none of the three cops is taller than five-foot-eight. In a force of mostly tall, burly men, the nickname is appropriate. But they pride themselves on being as tough as the next guy.

"A few times we tackled some big guys and we got hurt a little bit," says Besmer. "The lieutenant said, 'Maybe I'm going to put a big guy in and take one of you guys out. We told

DeStasio slumps on the steps behind a Times Square theater, her "belongings" at her side. Sometimes she passes the time by deciding what to serve for dinner the next day. Occasionally, she dozes off. (Carl Glassman)

him, 'Hey, listen, look at the statistics. The big guys get hurt just as much. As a matter of fact, we found out that we get hurt less than the big guys.' They didn't change us after that."

Despite their confidence, the threesome admits to getting into some tight spots. Jerry was working as a decoy when he saw a man run with a pocketbook into Central Park. "I chased him, but my back-up team didn't see me because it was dark. The guy was a lot larger than I am and there was a tussle over my gun. I got him face down and I had his hands spread—I was putting the handcuffs on him behind his back. The next thing I know he turned around facing me. We both got hold of my revolver. I was trying to pull it up and he was pulling it down. I thought I'd had it. I took the butt of it, turned it, and cracked him in the face with it. I kept hitting him until he finally turned it loose.

"When I wear a jacket now, I carry two guns. One at my belt and the other at my ankle. You never know when you're going to walk into something, or something's going to happen. If you get in a gunfight it's better to have two. It only takes about two seconds to fire all the bullets in your gun. It's quicker to drop down and pull out another one than it is to reload."

Just how dangerous is the job of cruising the streets or lying in wait of a mugger? That was the subject of discussion one night in the Munchkins' rickety unmarked car. It began with a simple, bold statement by Rice.

"I don't consider my job dangerous," he said.

"But how many people would approach someone on the street they think has a gun?" he was asked.

"That's my job," Rice shot back. "That's what they pay me to do. Besides, I've got *two* guns."

"But how did you feel the first time you did it?" Besmer asked him.

"The first time I took a gun away from somebody? I wet my pants."

"Over the years it's just like a ballplayer," Besmer explained. "His first major league game he's going to be nervous and scared as hell. But as you keep going along and doing the same thing over and over again, you start getting a feeling of confidence in yourself that you're not going to get hurt. It took me a couple of months before I first started to settle down."

"I'm conscious that the element of danger exists," says Bronte. "I daresay that if I was involved in an incident that resulted in something serious happening to one of these guys or someone I knew real well it could shake me up." But would he quit his job? "I make $25,000 a year, I have a very lucrative pension system, my medical care is all paid for. Frankly I don't think I could earn that money doing something else." Then the detective added with a laugh, "Of course, if someone offered me a fellowship or a chair at Columbia University for what I know, I'd consider it."

TEST PILOTS
and
ASTRONAUTS

If you are looking for perfect safety you will do well to sit on a fence and watch the birds, but if you really wish to learn you must mount a machine and become acquainted with its tricks by actual trial.

— Wilbur Wright

Barely one lifetime has passed since a powered plane first lifted a man into the air. From that historic December morning in 1903, when Orville Wright took his and brother Wilbur's homemade biplane for a sputtering 12-second ride above the sands of Kitty Hawk, North Carolina, men and women have dared to stretch the thresholds of flight, forever pushing higher, faster, and farther. In only 66 years,

Judy Resnik is suspended in a parachute harness during one of many training exercises that teach Space Shuttle astronauts how to survive an emergency ejection from their craft. (NASA)

their efforts soared from Kitty Hawk to the moon. Along the way, more than a few aviators lost their lives flight-testing the latest winged machine.

Test pilots of today share little in common with the somewhat mythical fliers of 40 and 50 years ago—their courageous counterparts who suited up in cloth helmets and leather jackets, threw scarves around their necks, and cast planes and caution to the wind. There was no sophisticated testing equipment to measure a new plane's limitations, no computers to help with airborne decisions.

Bill Dana, who's been a National Aeronautics and Space Administration (NASA) test pilot since 1959, recalls that the men he first worked with had little formal education in engineering, but were good pilots and, perhaps most important, had lots of self-confidence. Today, test pilots can discover and practice handling potential problems in experimental airplanes by "flying" simulators — computerized cockpits identical to the real thing, right down to the views seen through the windows. But back then the only way to see what a plane could do was to take it into the air and find out. "They'd build a plane that looked about right and go out and fly it," Dana recalls. "If it got back they'd keep modifying it until it was perfected."

Dana considers himself luckier than most of his fellow pilots because he counts only one time in his career when he thought he would be killed. "I got into a high-speed porpoise in a fighter I was testing at low altitude — the airplane just went up and down out of control to where I thought the wings were coming off. I let loose of the stick to eject and as soon as I did I discovered that I was the guy who was causing the problem. The airplane smoothed right out and I brought it back and landed it."

Dana has known men who did not make it back. But in the familiar refrain of so many who lead dangerous lives, he says he can't afford to let it affect him. "Within two or three months after I started flying I learned that there were some losses in this game. You feel sorry that you've lost your best friends, but you can't dwell too much on the 'what ifs' or you just wouldn't stay in this line of work."

Probably the most challenging and exciting plane that any test pilot has flown is the X-15. At its fastest, it traveled 4,520 miles an hour— more than six and a half times faster than the speed of sound. At its maximum, it climbed to an altitude of 67 miles—more than nine times higher than a commercial jet. To develop that kind of power, the X-15, which looked more like a missile than an airplane, was virtually a flying fuel tank. When its tank was completely filled, 20,000 pounds of the rocket's 34,000 pounds was rocket fuel. To conserve it, the X-15 didn't take off like a normal airplane, but was carried into the air beneath the wing of the B-52, a large bomber. Once launched on its own, the rocket's engine burned for only 80 to 120 sec-

Test pilot Bill Dana. (NASA)

onds. Then, like a glider, it returned to Earth without power.

Only 12 men (one was killed) ever flew the *X-15* when it was being tested at Edwards Air Force Base, California, between 1959 and 1968. Dana was one of them. For every hour he spent flying the rocket, he practiced 50 hours in a simulator. Dana's description of what a flight was like explains why there could be no room for error.

"Usually we'd come in about six o'clock in the morning and fly practice flights in a fighter — an *F-104* — just going out and practicing power-off landings [no engine running] to all possible dry lakes in the area we might have to land at that day.

"When we came back from flying the fighter, we'd climb into a van where a number of technicians would strap us into our pressure suits and helmets. I felt like a guinea pig because they would attach instruments to us to find out the physiological effects of high speed. There were leads glued all over you and sometimes they shaved hair off your chest. I guess that was the only part of it I didn't like.

"We'd climb into the *X-15* and maybe spend 30 minutes going through every switch in the cockpit, making sure that every switch and lever and valve was in the proper position for pre-launch. Then they'd close the canopy on the airplane and fire up the eight engines on the *B-52*. We'd taxi out and take off and maybe fly an hour into Nevada and then turn around

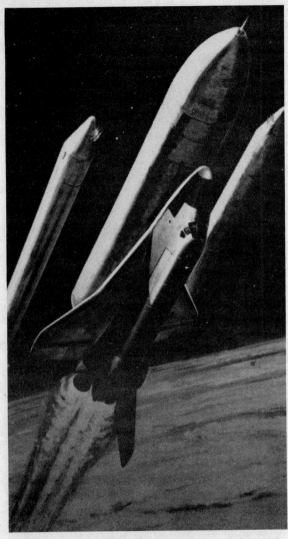

Artist's conception of the Space Shuttle as it jettisons its two solid rocket boosters at an altitude of 27 miles—and a speed of 3,213 miles an hour. (NASA)

and point back to Edwards and launch subsonically (below the sound barrier) at about 45,000 feet.

"As soon as we [the *X-15*] dropped off the wing, we lit the engine of a big rocket and things happened fast. We were thrown into the back of the seat and in about 90 seconds we'd climbed to an altitude of 130,000 feet at Mach 6 [six times the speed of sound] with about a 4g acceleration.

"After the engine shut down, we were weightless for two to three minutes. To reenter the atmosphere, you'd have to put about 5 g's down into your seat as you made your reentry and come back to level flight. Five g's is within human capability. It takes practice but it's not a superhuman task. The problem is you're pretty much pinned in your seat. Your arms and feet weigh five times as much as they do normally so you just can't move them around much. And you're working in a very constrained atmosphere. It takes a lot of physical effort to do anything.

"In 11 minutes we'd traveled 250 or 300 miles and made a dead-stick [power-off] landing. *That* was exciting."

Today, there are still some risks in being a test pilot. But the most sophisticated and daring planes are first flown remotely from the ground, with the pilot behind the controls of a duplicate cockpit, looking at a TV picture sent down from cameras in the flying aircraft. One of the most dramatic examples on the horizon is the *HiMAT* fighter, so maneuverable that it will be able to make turns twice as sharp as any other fighter. The resulting gravity force will be so powerful that the pilot may have to fly the plane lying down. But before anyone takes the fighter up, a half-size model will be flown from the ground.

Test pilots who are working with planes like the *HiMAT* are more scientists than daredevils. Their advanced knowledge of aerodynamic engineering, computer science, and flight analysis doesn't make them better pilots than their predecessors. But it makes them better test pilots. "The days of the scarf in the wind are gone," says Dana.

The *Space Shuttle*, scheduled for its first manned flight in 1980, will do what no other spacecraft has done before: blast into the earth's orbit like a rocket, and sail back home like a glider.

John Young and Robert Crippen will do what no other men have done before: Fly it.

NASA has never been so bold as to send up an unproven spacecraft with men inside. To the layman, the risks seem a little unnerving. After all, no one knows exactly what will happen to the oddly configured craft when it breaks the sound barrier, and shock waves knock the ship about. And the landing, too, appears dangerous, since the orbiter (the manned airplanelike section) will be a powerless glider. If there's a miscalculation in its

John Young, commander of the first Space Shuttle flight, sits at the controls of a computerized Shuttle simulator. Young will have "flown" the simulator many times before actually blasting into space. (NASA)

landing approach, there'll be no chance to circle for another try.

In time, computers will be making most of the on-board decisions. But for Young and Crippen and other pioneer *Shuttle* pilots, the mission is theirs to make — or break.

Does it take a daring man to be first behind the controls?

"Heck, no," says Young, who has already made four trips into space, and walked on the moon. "I don't go downtown on the freeway anymore if I can avoid it."

Crippen, who has never flown in space but as a test pilot logged more than 3,800 hours in jets, goes a step further. "Basically," he says, "I'm a chicken."

A chicken? Hardly. Young and Crippen, like most astronauts and successful test pilots, are overly modest. But they're also convinced that the element of risk is comparatively small when flying a spacecraft that costs an estimated $9.5 billion and countless man-hours to develop. For what the country won't see when the crew completes its mission are the years they spent getting ready, the 60 to 80 hours a week of training. Much of that time has been spent in simulators, learning what to do in case any of a multitude of system failures arise.

"I don't think I'm taking any chances," says Young. "The fact is that if I didn't think we could do these things and get away with them you wouldn't get me on top of that rocketship."

Crippen concurs. "There are always things

that are going to go wrong on a first flight. That's why we spend so much time preparing for malfunctions."

For John Young, and some of the other astronauts who will fly *Shuttle* missions in the future, the orbiter is not just a new toy to take into space—it's a piece of their own creation. Young had barely returned home from his 11-day *Apollo 16* moon mission in April 1972, when he and other astronauts began work on the early design and development of the *Shuttle,* including its living quarters, cockpit configuration, design for extra-vehicular activity (EVA—tasks performed outside the ship while it's in space), and flying and handling qualities. So between their contributions in engineering and thousands of hours of training, being an astronaut means a good deal more than taking an occasional ride into space.

"All the public is really seeing are the end results, which are fairly dramatic and important," says astronaut Fred Haise, who also joined the *Shuttle* program in 1972 and who test-landed the orbiter prototype, the *Enterprise,* in its first manned drop from a Boeing 747. "The problem the layman has is that he does not understand the details of the machine. So he's missing seventy-five percent of it, or maybe even more. I've spent years working on the *Space Shuttle.* How much have I flown? Not very much. And even when I go on a space flight it won't be for very long—just four, five, or six days. It won't be anything compared

105

to the work I've put in. To me, that's the satisfaction."

The *Space Shuttle* will be a first, and in a way
also a last, for NASA plans no new manned
space vehicles for at least through the 1990s.
Eventually growing to a fleet of five, the shut-
tles will be NASA's equivalent to the pick-up
truck, capable of routinely hauling cargo the
size of a Greyhound bus into space. In its huge
payload bay, the orbiter will lift tomorrow's
satellites into orbit, or whisk them *out* of orbit
for repairs. It will also carry into orbit spacelabs
and telescopes that will extend our view of the
universe seven times farther than we can see
from Earth.

And just maybe, John Young hopes, the
Shuttle will be useful in still another way. "I
wouldn't want to bet that we don't get a chance
to go back to the moon. When the *Space Shuttle*
comes on line in the mid-'80s, you could hook a
couple of modules together in it and do direct
trips to the moon very cheaply."

The astronauts who pilot future *Shuttle*
flights will have much the same background as
those who commanded past manned missions:
former test pilots with degrees in aeronautical
engineering. But once the *Shuttle* gets past the
testing phase, it will carry up to five non-pilot
astronauts, known as mission specialists, who
will be charged with carrying out a wide variety
of *Shuttle* missions, from manufacturing opti-
cal glass to launching satellites.

Judy Resnik, a 30-year-old electrical en-

To practice maneuvering in weightlessness, Astronaut Robert Crippen put on his spacesuit and went underwater. (NASA)

gineer, will become one of them. In April 1978, she began a two-year training program that will lead to a job as mission specialist and possibly the distinction of becoming the first American woman in space.

"I'm not here to get my name in books or to make a name as the first woman astronaut," Resnik says emphatically. "I'm here to contribute to the space program and do the best job that I can."

For now, that means spending most of her time in classrooms, or working on "technical assignments" with other technicians. Then there are the 15 hours a month of required flight time in the back seat of a *T-38* jet, and staying in shape by jogging and lifting weights every day after work.

"It's not a glamour job like people imagine it is," says Resnik.

Early in her training Resnik underwent the demanding task of learning emergency abort procedures. To practice landing in water, she was towed behind a powerboat, harnessed to a kite-like parasail, and lifted some 500 feet into the air. Then the line was released and she floated back into the water, where she had to get rid of her gear, blow up a liferaft, light flares, and go through helicopter rescue. Learning the emergency procedures, she says, "instilled a lot of self-confidence in me. When they tell you what to do it's one thing. When you actually go through the simulated motions, it's a lot different."

Resnik feels that she and the other astronauts are so well-trained to cope with every conceivable malfunction that "it does not enter any of our minds that it is dangerous. The world might think it is. We don't. I think something's dangerous only if you're not prepared for it, or you don't have control over it, or you can't think through how to get yourself out of the problem."

Judy Resnik doesn't question the safety of flying in space, but neither does she discuss the issue with those, like her parents, whom she'll be leaving behind on Earth. "Nobody's ever come out and said I was weird or crazy or 'Gee, don't you think that's a little risky?' I don't know if they think that. I also don't care."

As self-assured as astronauts and NASA officials may sound, they probably will never allow themselves to be quite as confident as they were on the afternoon of April 11, 1970, when Captain James A. Lovell, Jr., John L. Swigert, Jr., and Fred Haise left the Earth for the moon. Unknown to anyone that day, the crew was headed not to the lunar surface but to nightmarish near-tragedy.

America's first two trips to the moon had been so successful that the world was practically taking this one for granted. The first 55 hours of the trip were, indeed, uneventful. In fact, a Houston flight controller radioed to the astronauts that they were "putting us to sleep down here." Nothing could go wrong. And if something did, there was a back-up system and still more back-up systems to handle it.

At 9:05 P.M. on April 13, the moon was 45,000 miles away from the astronauts, and Earth five times that distance behind them. That moment, the spacecraft shook. Warning lights flashed. "We've got a problem," Lovell reported to Mission Control. His voice was even, but the astronauts knew that something was very wrong. It would take 15 minutes before anyone realized that one of the spacecraft's two oxygen tanks, which supplied power to the Command Module's life support system, had exploded. It would take an hour before NASA acknowledged that nothing could be done to repair the damage and even longer for anyone to believe that the source of the failure was in the spacecraft itself. They could only imagine that a meteor had hit it.

The ship was divided into three main parts, or "modules." The Command Module, in which the astronauts were riding, was the vehicle for carrying the men into the moon's orbit and back to Earth. Once in lunar orbit, two astronauts would descend in a Lunar Module (LM—pronounced "lem") to the moon's surface while Swigert continued to orbit in the Command Module. When Haise and Lovell completed their expedition, they would link the LM back up with the Command Module and fly home. A third section of the spacecraft, called the Service Module, contained, among other things, the oxygen tanks—the contents of

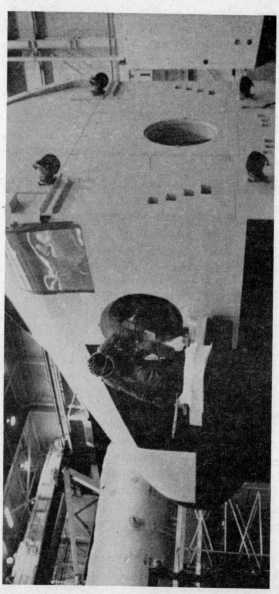

Astronauts Young and Crippen rehearse emergency exit procedures from a mockup of the Shuttle cabin. (NASA)

which were now spewing into space.

As power quickly bled from the Command Module, it became apparent that the astronauts' only hope for survival was to turn the Lunar Module into a kind of lifeboat, which they hoped would provide the thrust and the guidance to get the ship around the moon and back to the Earth's outer atmosphere.

Since NASA's army of engineers never anticipated a failure that the astronauts couldn't fix in space, no one was prepared for such a contingency. As Swigert later wrote: "If somebody had thrown that at us in the simulator, we'd have said, 'Come on, you're not being realistic.'" As a result, the LM's air and water would have to be stretched three times farther; and its power would need to be cut in half in order to make it back. For the astronauts, that meant surviving four days of perpetual cold in an unheated spacecraft, and dehydration brought on by conserving the water supply.

But before they went anywhere in the LM lifeboat, the crew first had to get the lifeless spacecraft "powered up," a procedure sketched out in a two-hour-long checklist. The men had barely begun the switch-over when Mission Control informed them that they had only 15 minutes of power left in the Command Module. It was up to LM commander Haise and the LM Systems Officer who monitored the module in Houston to improvise a quick set of steps that would get the module functioning and safely on its way. The men weren't trained for the emergency, but their intimate knowledge of the craft paid off. With hasty precision, the Command Module was shut down and the LM was powered up successfully. The first step of the emergency plan had worked. Now the crew had only a trip around the moon and more than a quarter of a million miles to go.

The next four days were treacherous for the astronauts and nerve-grinding for the ground controllers, whose every decision could mean the difference between the men returning safely or not returning at all. Precisely where and how much, for example, should they try to correct the ship's misguided course, when each redirecting "burn" of the LM's main rocket meant the loss of precious power. How would the crew escape suffocating in their own exhaled carbon dioxide? What about tropical storm Helen, which the weathermen said was heading straight for the astronauts' new splashdown point? As soon as one problem was solved, another one crept up.

While most of the decision-making was done from the ground, the astronauts had to remain alert to carry out the flight controller's complicated instructions and sometimes make life-or-death choices of their own. It wasn't easy, expecially since sleep was nearly impossible. As the spacecraft rolled back and forth, blinding sunlight flashed onto the faces of the men trying to doze off. When one of the astronauts closed the shade, the temperature of the Command Module "bedroom" dipped to around 40 degrees. It stayed that way for the rest of the flight. The men could have warmed up by donning their spacesuits but, afraid they'd become clumsy, they remained only in shirtsleeves.

The astronauts could not sleep more than three hours a day, and for the better part of two days they had no sleep at all. Lovell was becoming so fatigued that he made mistakes in keeping the ship on course. To make matters worse, a beeping sound, coming from the third stage of the Saturn rocket that had launched them, was being picked up on the radio. Lovell and the flight controllers could barely hear each other. Swigert spilled water on his shoes and they wouldn't dry, refrigerating his feet for days. Haise developed a kidney infection and he once shivered for four hours straight.

The mission that began with relatively little public notice now gripped the attention of the world. No science-fiction fantasy could match the real-life drama of three men up there— somewhere—soaring uncertainly through the ominous void. Somehow, the infinite unknown of space and the incomprehensible wizardry of space travel made the astronauts' plight seem all the more terrible. In their Earthbound helplessness, millions prayed.

The astronauts themselves were either too busy or too worn out to worry much about whether they would get back alive. Looking back, Fred Haise says: "If I had to describe the emotions I felt as things progressed, they

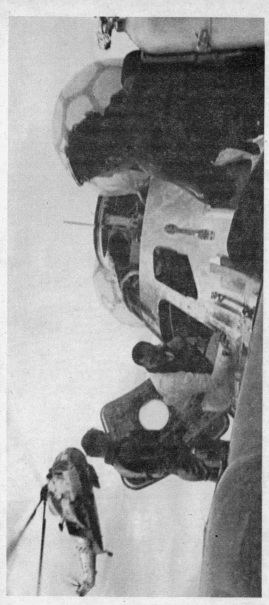

The crew of *Apollo 13* came perilously close to being lost in space. Navy frogmen helped with the recovery of the three astronauts after splash-down. John L. Swigert was the first man out. (NASA)

would have ranged from disappointment to discomfort. A lot of years had gone into doing this thing, a lot of training in geology, lunar surface work, LM operation to land and launch again, and of course it went out the window. It was a failure. The discomfort came because of the cold. It was very much like outdoor survival, only we weren't outdoors.... It got pretty grim."

With their spacecraft accelerating toward Earth (from 3,000 miles an hour to its peak speed of 24,000 miles an hour) the planet grew larger and larger in the window of their little Lunar Module, and the time approached for reentry into the Earth's atmosphere. The reentry checklist, a phonebook-size schedule that took three months to prepare, would be thrown out and replaced by a checklist the flight controllers improvised in three days.

The LM was useless as an Earth reentry vehicle because it would incinerate in the 5,000 degree heat generated during its fall through the Earth's atmosphere. Only the Command Module, with its special heat shield, could protect the crew. Fortunately, the module's reentry system was unharmed by the oxygen tank explosion. But no one was certain about the heat shield. When the astronauts jettisoned the Service Module into space, they got their first look at the extensive damage. "It's really a mess," Haise told the ground. Everyone knew how close the oxygen tanks were to the Command Module's heat shield, but no one uttered a word of concern. If the explosion had rendered the shield useless, there simply was nothing anyone could do about it.

There were other uncertainties, too. Could the Command Module's electrical system be revived after three lifeless days in the cold of space? And could the ship find its way into the narrow one-and-a-half-degree-wide reentry corridor at just the right angle?

Somehow, everything worked. Even tropical storm Helen obliged the crew by missing the landing site. The Module dropped safely into calm Pacific waters.

Physicians who examined the crew aboard the rescuing aircraft carrier found them to be in worse shape than any other returning astronauts. Their reflexes were slow, their legs unsteady. But they were home.

WAR CORRESPONDENTS

Unfortunately, there is almost always work somewhere in the world for the war correspondent. His stories and pictures are such everyday fixtures in newspapers, magazines, and on TV that we tend to treat battlefront news as casually as the weather report. But behind those daily estimates of casualties, and accounts of sniper attacks, troop movements and civilian suffering, there is the hidden story of the journalist himself. Protected only by paper-thin press credentials, he must get close enough to the fighting to sort facts out of chaos. In the process, his life often becomes as endangered and his experiences as dramatic as the war he reports.

Figures on the number of reporters who have died in various wars are hard to come by. But in Vietnam alone, 45 correspondents were killed and another 18 were reported missing and are presumed dead.

Journalists cover wars for different reasons. Some thrive on the action, even go out of their way to cover it. Others are foreign correspondents caught in the crossfire when fighting flares up in their regions. Following are the accounts of three war reporters: Alvin Rosenfeld, a former television correspondent; John Smith, news cameraman; and Mike Ross, wire service reporter.

During his nearly 25 years as a foreign correspondent, Alvin Rosenfeld covered four wars between Egypt and Israel as well as conflicts on the Indian subcontinent, Cyprus, Algeria, and "various and other upsets hither and yon."

In 1964, Rosenfeld was shot in the face while covering the communal war in Cyprus. Although he lost the sight in his left eye and hearing in his left ear, he returned overseas the following year and covered more wars, including the Arab-Israeli war.

"One thing you have to understand about war correspondents is that they always believe, even more than soldiers do, that the bullet's not for them. It isn't their war, they don't have guns in their hands, so they don't think they are vulnerable.

"When I first went to Israel I didn't envision myself as beginning a long career as a war correspondent. No one, in their wildest dreams, would have thought there would be a half a dozen Middle Eastern wars in 30 years. But I was very interested in the area and I liked working overseas.

"The layman probably thinks that the life of a foreign correspondent is glamorous and fun. And it is. But it involves a tremendous amount of boot-work, incredibly long hours—12 to 18 hours a day—and seeing extremely unpleasant sights. Also, it involves risking your life and it involves human emotions. No matter how tough you think you are—and you have to be because otherwise you would fall apart—you are affected by what you see.

"In all the wars I've been in, I knew of only one guy who couldn't hack it, who had been through too much. It is common, though, for guys to have to leave temporarily because the strain becomes too much. After the Arab-Israeli Six-Day War, when I worked day and night for two or three weeks, NBC sent me out of the country for about 10 days. I had reached the edge of weariness.

"Wars have a lasting effect on everybody in one way or another. There are scenes you never forget. For me, those days are very vivid. They were among the most exciting days of my life. They were horrible sometimes and very exciting other times. Even tragedy can be riveting.

"There are various reasons why people want to cover war. It's vital and significant, it's action and it is dramatic news with good story possibilities. You're one of the last of the inde-

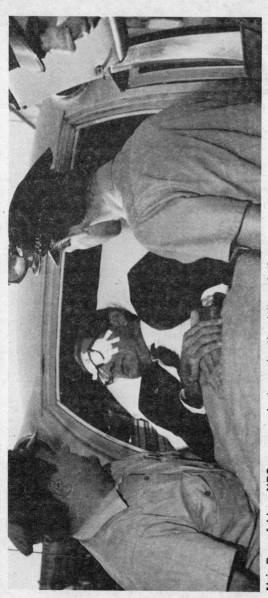

Alvin Rosenfeld, an NBC correspondent covering the civil war in Cyprus, returning home after being shot in the eye. Rosenfeld lost his sight in the eye and hearing in his left ear, but continued to cover wars for nine more years. (NBC Photo)

pendents. You have to make decisions on your own. There isn't anybody else who can make them for you. And you have to make them fast. In a war, you frequently have a choice of places to go every day. You have to decide, 'Am I going to go to this section of the front or that section?'; 'Where's the action most likely to be?' This is particularly true in television. If a printed-word journalist is not at a scene where something important has happened, he can frequently recoup by getting one of his colleagues to provide a fill-in. In television, if you and your camera aren't there, tough luck. You have lost the story forever.

"You want to be where the action is because you want to see what is going on and to have the most dramatic footage. We used to go out to the Suez Canal—a 12-hour drive in each direction. Why did we go? To be able to say, 'Here we are on the banks of the Canal.' And to supplement what the camera saw with description and analysis.

"I saw prisoners, I saw and smelled death, but I didn't see ignorant armies clashing by night. I saw relatively small-scale operations. In the end I was sickened by it, but when I was a lot younger I saw it as a job—a job I thought I could do well.

"During the '73 Arab-Israeli war, I remembered seeing swollen corpses—they happened to have been Arab soldiers—and I remember the pain, the nausea, and the disgust I felt over the loss of so much human life.

122

Following a Viet Cong attack on an American air base at Khe Sahn, CBS News cameraman John Smith films the rescue of wounded soldiers—though he himself is seriously wounded at the time. Note the blood below his ear. (Photo courtesy of John Smith)

"Your desire as a war correspondent is to say: 'Hey world, look at the bravery, look at the madness, look at the magnificence.' All these things are elements of war. You cover riots in New York or Washington, you cover death in Teheran. It doesn't make you happy. But it's part of the job. And it's challenging because it's all terribly, terribly confusing. How in the world are you going to figure out what's happening?

"The army you travel with views you as both their enemy and their friend. You are of tremendous value because you show the bravery of individual units and their accomplishments. You can be a threat also, because you can reveal information they don't want revealed—a defeat, a type of weapon used, a position of a given unit or its plans.

"The day I was injured, my cameraman and I were riding along the northern coast of Cyprus looking for a story. The preceding day the mainland Turkish air force had intervened in the communal warfare and bombed a village. There were rumors of more bombings, so we went to investigate. The Greek Cypriots, for whatever reason, didn't want us to. They stopped us at a road block and everybody turned back to Nicosia, the capital. My cameraman and I had heard a rumor that there were war refugees living in tents near a side road—a good human-interest story. We found them and then used the detour in an effort to bypass the Greek roadblock. We were going merrily along until we came to a new roadblock, manned by one Greek Cypriot soldier. We said, 'Hey, foreign press,' and he didn't stop us.

"Normally, neither the Greeks nor the Turks fired at civilian rental automobiles because the only people who were crazy enough to drive them near the battlefront were correspondents. We were considered neutral and potentially valuable. So we felt totally safe as we drove along the road. Then one shot was fired. Whether it was a ricochet or fired deliberately, I don't know. But I was hit. At the time I didn't realize that I was seriously wounded. You reach a point, I suppose, which is beyond pain. I didn't feel any severe pain. I wasn't in agony. I was uncomfortable. And I was disoriented. But I wasn't in pain. It was my bad luck, however, that the little incident occurred just before dusk, and we were in a no-man's land for 10 or 11 hours before being rescued.

"A war correspondent, compared to a reporter covering city hall or the U.S. Senate, sees only a small portion of what is happening. A war in modern terms involves so many different things—battles here, there, and the other place, diplomatic action, supply situations, air action—that a correspondent is only seeing a tiny window on a big picture. But you never forget the view, grim as it is."

John Smith was a news cameraman at a Nashville, Tennessee, TV station for seven years before contracting with CBS in 1966 to cover the Vietnam War. He was seriously wounded at Khe Sahn, but after four weeks of recuperating in the United States, he returned to the action. At the end of his 18-month contract, Smith got back his old job in Nashville, but the excitement of working overseas drew him again to Vietnam, and four times he returned to war zones in Southeast Asia. Later, Smith joined CBS's Atlanta bureau. In 1978, at the age of 39, he found himself once more in the throes of war, this time covering the uprising against Nicaraguan dictator Anastasio Somoza Debayle and his National Guard. Smith, along with other members of the Atlanta bureau, went to Nicaragua three times, replacing crews who found the job too dangerous. He won a prestigious National Press Photographers Association award for his camera work there.

"I read an ad in *TV Guide* on Thanksgiving day, 1966, saying that all the networks needed technicians, correspondents, reporters, soundmen, to work in Vietnam. By the next week I got up enough courage to call New York and ask about it. They said why don't you come to our office tomorrow and talk to us. Less than six weeks later I was in Vietnam and under fire.

"I was with a reporter all the time. You have to work together as a team. If he sees something he wants, he tells me, and if I see something I like I'll shoot it and tell him about it later. I guess I'm in more danger than a reporter. When everyone else is ducking, I have to be shooting. It's the only way to get a picture. You can't do a lot of thinking, you've got to go by gut feeling. If you sat down and tried to analyze every scene and situation, deciding whether it was too dangerous to shoot, you'd never get anything done.

"At first, it didn't occur to me that I might get killed. I went for 13 months in Vietnam and refused to wear a flak jacket or a helmet. I always said I couldn't see through the viewfinder if I was wearing a helmet. I was convinced that, since I was neutral, it couldn't happen to me. I never even ducked when we were being hit by incoming fire.

"We went into the DMZ one time and it was 125 degrees and they would not let us off the carrier unless we carried a helmet and flak jacket. And I carried it—I carried it as far as the beach and then I tossed it onto the sand. I had no fear of anything happening to me. I was stupid.

"For one thing, in Vietnam the camera looked like a weapon to many Viet Cong. They were unsophisticated and it could have looked like a grenade launcher or anything else.

"On February 1st, 1968, we were at Khe Sahn with a reporter named Igor Orinessoff, our correspondent from Japan. We were standing next to each other at the regimental headquarters when a couple of mortar rounds came in, landing about 100 yards away. A small piece hit Igor in the throat. Three millimeters forward and it would have gotten his larynx. Three millimeters backwards and it would have gotten his spinal cord. It was still a hell of a wound, and that's when I realized it could happen to me. After that I started ducking.

"We would sometimes reach a combat zone by hitching a ride on a *C-130* transport plane. The plane would land on this steel-plated runway, make a 180-degree turn, kick off the cargo out the rear, and then we'd jump out after that. Then, without ever stopping, the plane revved up and tried to get out of there immediately. Four of us from CBS, reporter Don Webster, my soundman D. V. Mai, and a producer, Russ Bensley, from New York, landed at Khe Sahn that way when the Marines were surrounded. As we got off the back of the plane, my soundman was caught in the prop-wash and he just rolled out like a tumbleweed on the western desert. He was bruised so badly that he couldn't walk. Bensley then became my soundman.

"We did several stories around there and had just finished filming a conversation with a soldier from Tennessee when we heard a crash. A *C-123* aircraft had tried to take off when a mortar round was dropped right in front of it, causing the plane to go off the runway into a ditch, turn on its side, and catch on fire. We went down to take a picture, standing among about a hundred other guys. We were such a beautiful target that the enemy dropped two more mortar rounds right quick. A mortar round is nothing but an anti-personnel weapon, designed specifically to hurt people. It hit right behind us on the runway and splattered like an egg hitting concrete. It got me and Bensley up and down our backs. It felt like someone had just taken a handful of rocks and thrown them at my back. I couldn't really tell it was serious until I reached around and got a handful of blood. We crawled under an ambulance. Another round or two came in. When it seemed like it had stopped, we got out and finished filming the rest of the rescue of the plane on fire. We gave the film to the reporter, and then went to separate aid stations. The one I went to said I wasn't hurt, that the wounds were all superficial. They put some bandages on me and I went back to Da Nang, to process the film and satellite it to New York.

"From there I went to the Air Force Hospital because the bandages wouldn't stay on and I was getting blood on everything. They took X rays and then told me they didn't know where the shrapnel had gone, whether it was in my lung or intestine or liver. Up until then I hadn't felt any pain, but when I heard that, I about fainted. I was helicoptered to the Navy Hospital, where it was just like *M*A*S*H* on TV — a regular operating theater. They took out a big hunk in my back, a big hunk in my leg, and altogether there were 13 wounds. In the middle of the operation, while the doctor was digging around in me he stopped and helped the guy next to me who had gone into cardiac arrest. He had a .50-calibre wound right through his chest. Somehow, they brought him back to life.

"The next day CBS sent a plane in with a crew to replace us and take me back to Saigon. That night, the Viet Cong were attacking a helicopter base near the hospital where I had been, and a round that fell short hit the hospital. Bensley was still there, lying in his bed, and got a piece of rocket round and a piece of quantas hut in his stomach while he was lying there unable to move.

"I went back to Nashville, to see my own doctor, and four weeks later I was back in Vietnam.

"I returned because I wanted to make sure that I could. If you fall off a bicycle or get thrown by a horse you want to know you can ride again. Also, I loved the country over there. Loved the climate. When you can get papaya for breakfast and you don't have to wear a coat during the day, that's paradise for me.

"Probably the one drawback of the job is that you have to be so detached from everything, to be an impartial observer to whatever is happening. Yet you have to have a feeling for your pictures. Whether you're photographing a corpse or a politician you don't like, or the most revolting thing you can think of, you still make it a great, spectacular, or award-winning picture, if you can. Your name is on that tape. So you want it to be the right focus, the right exposure, the right composition. Nevertheless, there have been a lot of shots that

130

were too gruesome to put on the air.

"In 1978, I went to Nicaragua three times to replace people who didn't want to stay there any longer. They didn't like being shot at.

"It wasn't a controlled war and there was a lot of aimless fire coming down the street — bullets with nobody's name on them—looking for a random target.

"We stayed in Managua, which was rather far removed from where the fighting was going on. One morning, reporter Bruce Hall, soundman J.W. Womack, and I left about six o'clock and drove by taxi for two hours to Matagalpa, using our credentials to get us through roadblocks. Everyone was leaving the town and they all had white flags on their car antennas. Being the only traffic going toward town gave us a little bit of an eerie feeling. The closer to town we got the more fires we began to see and the more we were stopped. Then we'd see people on foot walking away from town. A constant stream of people, kids and old women, everyone carrying a white flag, with everything they could carry on their backs.

"We walked across the bridge, into the heart of downtown, and everywhere the streets were deserted. A reporter came out and told us where the rebels, called the Sandinistas, were.

"The Sandinistas were these kids — really just kids. Some of them had masks on. They had 30-ought-6 rifles, some .22s and quite a few handguns. Some of them were making Molotov cocktails and putting up sandbags.

UPI correspondent Mike Ross, whose life was often in danger during the two years he covered the Lebanese Civil War.

They had blocked the streets off by burning stuff in the intersections. We spent some time there, interviewing one of these kids and taking pictures of the others looking down at the National Guard, their enemy, who were roughly three-quarters of a mile down the street.

"It was obvious that we had only a limited amount of time to stay with the rebels. The National Guard had M-1s, M-14s, Israeli rifles, and tanks, and if we didn't get out before they attacked, we'd have gotten wiped out along with the rebels.

"We went back down the side of the river to the city square. We took pictures of the National Guard trying to get their tanks started and moving around. All this time there were stray bullets flying around. You didn't move across open streets without moving quickly. There were snipers at the ends of the streets and any time they saw someone move at the other end they would shoot.

"My soundman and I were standing in a doorway, with only my lens sticking out, when a ricochet came up. I don't know what it had hit off of, but it bounced off the metal door and hit me in the leg, stinging about like a bee sting. I found it on the ground and picked it up—my souvenir of Matagalpa. The ABC cameraman got hit the same way, only it hit the concrete first. Had the soundman or I been over just slightly, one of us could have been badly hurt.

"The reporter left, taking the first stuff back to Managua for the satellite feed, while the soundman and I stayed on and taped a little longer. At one point a National Guardsman was shot and blinded in the street. Apparently his unit was trained so that, no matter what, don't let the other side get your weapon. So this Guardsman was in the center of the street, crawling around in circles in mud and water trying to find his gun. He found it, brought it back, and they finally got him out.

"I photographed that and then we followed the ambulance back to the hospital and taped the medical teams working on the soldiers and wounded civilians. By then it was getting dark. We got back in the car and returned to Managua. The earlier piece that Bruce Hall brought back had already gone out in time for the Walter Cronkite evening news. They edited what we brought back into a piece for the morning news, and then that was satellited out.

"Early the next morning we got up and did it all again.

"I am very thankful that there are people who can work on assembly lines and do the same things time after time after time to put that car together for me to drive. I could never do that. I've got to do something different every day.

"The TV viewer may feel like he's seeing the same depressing picture of war every day, but to the cameraman no two days are the same. It's a different place and a different experience of being shot at each time. And people don't realize that it can be as big a job to get the pictures on the air as it is taking them. You have to get out of the combat area with the tape, and make the long journey back to town. Then you hope the equipment is working when you get it there to edit. Then you hope the satellite is working. Finally you wonder how much time the show is going to allow for it today. Are they going to take this two-minute piece and cut it down to a minute, or are they going to drop it altogether because the President said something more important?

"Getting your pictures under stress is partly a matter of luck, and partly a matter of timing. You've got to know when the President is going to get up and start speaking, or when the crowd is going to surge toward the car or when they're going to start throwing rocks or whatever. No matter what's going to happen, you have to anticipate it.

"I wouldn't mind going back to cover another war. But I can live fine without ever seeing another one. As a matter of fact, I wish they'd just do away with wars. I can find a good picture story here that's quite safe to shoot."

After graduating from college, Mike Ross and his friends hopped on motorcycles and headed down Central America's Pan American Highway. When the group ran out of highway and money — in Panama — everyone returned home except Ross, who stayed on to work for an English-language paper in the morning, and the tourist office in the afternoon. Some time later, Ross joined United Press International, a wire service used by many different papers, and his assignments have taken him to Brussels, Rome, and, in December of 1974, to Beirut. A few months after arriving there, the Lebanese Civil War broke out. For the next two years, Ross ended up covering that complex and brutal conflict, fought between Christian militias, Palestinians, and Syrians, with Libyans, Iraqis, and Egyptians joining in. By the time Ross left Beirut, in November 1976, the city was only a shell of the thriving metropolis he had seen when he had arrived.

"The whole city was a battlefield. A lot of the correspondents had also been in Vietnam—at least one of them as a soldier—and they all said the same thing. Beirut was much worse. In Vietnam you had an office and you had a battlefield and you more or less knew where the lines were. You could go to the battlefield, do your reporting, then come back to the office, have a stiff drink, and sit down and write your copy. But you couldn't do that in Beirut. You never knew where a bullet was going to come from or when a shell would come crashing in. It was a hazard just getting to the office. For about six months we had a couple of snipers inhabiting a rooftop a few hundred yards away from our office who would fire at the front door. So sometimes we had to crawl on our bellies just to get inside the office.

"The scariest thing for me—because it was the most impersonal and indiscriminate—was the sound of the shells. We were in the western side of town which was held by Palestinians and the leftist groups. And every day we took on 200 to 400 shells from the Christians.

"The shell fire came in at different times of the day and on different areas. They'd drop two or three shells and then stop for five minutes, long enough for people to come out from wherever they had sought cover, and then start again. It was indiscriminate shelling designed to terrorize, lower morale, and kill as many people as possible. You never really knew when it was safe to be outside and when it wasn't.

"I suppose if I'd been sitting in my office on my first day in Beirut and heard all the shells land, I'd have been on the next plane out. But as the war moved toward the city, I got accustomed to it.

"Fairly early in the war, 1,500 to 2,000 neighborhood thugs and revolutionary groups, under the command of the Popular Front for the Liberation of Palestine, launched an offensive attack on the hotel district. From the hotel roofs, one could have fire power over the entire area of West Beirut. My apartment at that time was right next to the Holiday Inn. The day the offensive started, I happened to have left early for the office. By the time I finished reporting this blood-and-guts story for American newspapers, I realized it was too dangerous to go home. The trouble was I had two cats in the house with nobody to feed them. I waited two days, hoping things would calm down. Finally, I decided the cats couldn't wait any longer and I would have to go get them. And, if I made it, I'd have a damn good feature story to boot.

"The streets between the office and my apartment were a no-man's land and no cab driver would take me there. My apartment was literally in the middle of the fighting. On one corner were the Christian Falangists and down the block were the Palestinians. En route, I was taken prisoner by a couple of 15-year-old kids with AK-47s (Russian rifles). At their headquarters, I was roughed up a bit and interrogated for some time, and accused of being a spy. At one point they put an unloaded gun to my head, trying to make me confess, and pulled the trigger.

"It was especially bad because I had a tape recorder with me—our audio department was always hungry for the sounds of explosions, machine-gun fire, and so on. Earlier in the day I had it on as I toured the destruction in another part of the city, and I also had picked up the conversations of some Falangists who were nearby. My captors wanted to hear the tape, and if they had, I would have been in worse trouble for consorting with the enemy. Fortunately, the kid who was trying to play the recorder couldn't quite figure out how it worked. Under the pretext of showing him, I erased most of the tape. After a few hours, I convinced them I was a friend of the revolution and I was released.

"From there I continued on to my house,

The Associated Press's Peter Arnett, who combined his skills as both a reporter and photographer, is among the best known—and luckiest—of all war correspondents. He survived 13 years of covering the Vietnam War. (Wide World Photo)

having to cross the other battle lines to get there. I finally reached home but I couldn't go through the entrance because it was too dangerous. So I went through another building, across a lot, and then shimmied up a basketball pole to get into a courtyard that led to the back entrance of my apartment. When I got there, the cats were terrified. I was on the fifth floor and the seventh and eighth floors were already on fire. I grabbed them, shoved them into a suitcase, and ran out again. In the process of shimmying back down the pole, one of the cats got out and started hanging from my shoulder for dear life. While that was happening, a sniper started taking pot shots at me — and came very close. I got back to my office, upset and shaken and bleeding. Then I had to sit down and start my regular shift.

"I don't think anybody ever really thought of leaving, though we had to send people out on vacation. We were working an average of 14 hours a day, seven days a week. After a few months of that, with all the anxieties of the situation, you were ready for the funny farm. You had to get away for a while. Toward the end of the war only three staffers were there at any given time, which was rough on the others because we had to work longer hours. But in a situation like that, where nothing was open, there was nothing to do except sit in your room — with or without electricity — and work.

"I went through a stage where I liked the excitement. Someone once said that there's nothing more stimulating than being shot at and missed. You go through that cowboy phase where you feel you're invincible, and you go out and try to prove that to yourself. It's a way of overcoming your fears. Fortunately for your health, you outgrow it after a while. In the case of most of us, the fear and tension sort of had a cumulative effect. In the beginning, you get shot at a few times—and missed—and you feel lucky. You think you can do anything. It happens again and again and after a while you begin to think it's about time your luck started to run out. Then you become more cautious.

"There are quite a few correspondents who thrive on war, a regular stable of them who follow wars around. Not too many of them were in Beirut, though. It scared most of them off. By and large the people who ended up covering the Lebanese War were the ones who happened to be there when it started.

"Why did I stay? Lord knows I wasn't there for the money. If it had been for that, I'd have become an accountant long ago. I don't want to sound pompous or even idealistic, but I did it because I believe it was an important story. I felt we had the obligation to cover it and I wanted to report that story as truthfully and accurately as I could."